AAT

Synoptic Assessment
Level 3
Advanced Diploma in
Accounting
Question Bank

Sixth edition 2021

ISBN 9781 5097 4210 3

(Previous ISBN 9781 5097 3453 5)

British Library Cataloguing-in-Publication Data
A catalogue record for this book is available
from the British Library

Published by

BPP Learning Media Ltd
BPP House, Aldine Place
142-144 Uxbridge Road
London W12 8AA

www.bpp.com/learningmedia

Printed in the United Kingdom

Your learning materials, published by BPP Learning
Media Ltd, are printed on paper obtained from
traceable sustainable sources.

Contents

Introduction

This is BPP Learning Media's AAT Question Bank for the *Advanced Diploma in Accounting Level 3 Synoptic Assessment*. It is part of a suite of ground-breaking resources produced by BPP Learning Media for AAT assessments.

This Question Bank contains these key features:

- Tasks corresponding to each assessment objective in the qualification specification and related task in the synoptic assessment. Some tasks in the Question Bank are designed for learning purposes, others are of assessment standard.

- In the main Question Bank there are occasionally links to online information (such as AAT ethics). These are there to assist you in the practice of these questions. In the real assessment, you will be supplied with a number of appendices which may include extracts of the AAT *Code of Professional Ethics* and/or VAT information. In the practice assessments in this book, you will have an appendix (at the back of this book) which is similar to that found in the real exam.

- AAT practice assessment 1 should be completed online to enable you to gain familiarity of the 'look' of the exam and how the additional information will be presented to you. This is available within the **Lifelong Learning Portal** on the AAT website.

The emphasis in all tasks and assessments is on the practical application of the skills acquired.

Test specification for the Level 3 synoptic assessment – Ethics for Accountants, Advanced Bookkeeping, Final Accounts Preparation and Management Accounting: Costing

Assessment method	Marking type	Duration of assessment
Computer based synoptic assessment	Partially computer/partial human marked	2 hours 30 minutes

Guidance from the AAT regarding completion of the Level 3 synoptic assessment

	Assessment objectives for the Level 3 synoptic assessment	Weighting
1	Demonstrate an understanding of the relevance of the ethical code for accountants, the need to act ethically in a given situation, and the appropriate action to take in reporting questionable behaviour	19%
2	Prepare accounting records and respond to errors, omissions and other concerns, in accordance with accounting and ethical principles and relevant regulations	15%
3	Demonstrate an understanding of the inter-relationship between the financial accounting and management accounting systems of an organisation and how they can be used to support managers in decision-making	16%
4	Apply ethical and accounting principles when preparing final accounts for different types of organisation, develop ethical courses of action and communicate relevant information effectively	19%
5	Analyse, interpret and report management accounting data	15%
6	Prepare financial accounting information, comprising extended trial balances and final accounts for sole traders and partnerships	16%
Total		**100%**

Approaching the assessment

When you sit the assessment it is very important that you follow the on screen instructions. This means you need to carefully read the instructions, both on the introduction screens and during specific tasks.

When you access the assessment you should be presented with an introductory screen with information similar to that shown below (taken from the introductory screen from one of the AAT's AQ2016 practice assessments for the *Advanced Diploma in Accounting Level 3 Synoptic Assessment*).

Assessment information

- You have **2 hours and 30 minutes** to complete this practice assessment.

- This assessment contains **6 tasks** and you should attempt to complete **every** task.

- Each task is independent. You will not need to refer to your answers to previous tasks.

- The total number of marks for this assessment is 80.

- Read every task carefully to make sure you understand what is required.

- Task 3 and Task 4 require extended writing as part of your response to these questions. You should make sure you allow adequate time to complete these tasks.

- Where the date is relevant, it is given in the task data.

- Both minus signs and brackets can be used to indicate negative numbers **unless** task instructions say otherwise.

- You must use a full stop to indicate a decimal point. For example, write 100.57 NOT 100,57 or 100 57

- You may use a comma to indicate a number in the thousands, but you don't have to. For example 10000 and 10,000 are both acceptable.

It is very important you read the instructions on the introductory screen and apply them in the assessment. You don't want to lose marks when you know the correct answer just because you have not entered it in the right format.

A full stop is needed to indicate a decimal point. We would recommend using minus signs to indicate negative numbers and leaving out the comma signs to indicate thousands, as this results in a lower number of key strokes and less margin for error when working under time pressure. Having said that, you can use whatever is easiest for you as long as you operate within the rules set out for your particular assessment.

You have to show competence throughout the assessment, and you should therefore complete all of the tasks. Don't leave questions unanswered.

In some assessments such as the synoptic assessment, written or complex tasks may be human marked. In this case you are given a blank space or table to enter your answer into. You are told in the assessments which tasks these are (**note.** there may be none if all answers are marked by the computer).

If these involve calculations, it is a good idea to decide in advance how you are going to lay out your answers to such tasks by practising answering them on a word document, and certainly you should try all such tasks in this Question Bank and in the AAT's environment using the assessment.

When asked to fill in tables, or gaps, never leave any blank even if you are unsure of the answer. Fill in your best estimate.

Note that for some assessments where there is a lot of scenario information or tables of data provided (eg tax tables), you may need to access these via 'pop-ups'. Instructions will be provided on how you can bring up the necessary data during the assessment.

Finally, take note of any task specific instructions once you are in the assessment. For example you may be asked to enter a date in a certain format or to enter a number to a certain number of decimal places.

Students will complete the synoptic assessment for the Advanced Diploma in Accounting in the 'locked down' environment of SecureClient in the same way as all other assessments.

It is strongly recommended that students visit the AAT Study Support Area and familiarise themselves with the software. There is a useful video 'How to sit an Advanced Diploma synoptic assessment' which explains how to navigate using the software. Do review this prior to sitting your assessment.

Grading

To achieve the qualification and to be awarded a grade, you must pass all the mandatory unit assessments, all optional unit assessments (where applicable) and the synoptic assessment.

The AAT Level 3 Advanced Diploma in Accounting will be awarded a grade. This grade will be based on performance across the qualification. Unit assessments and synoptic assessments are not individually graded. These assessments are given a mark that is used in calculating the overall grade.

How overall grade is determined

You will be awarded an overall qualification grade (Distinction, Merit, and Pass). If you do not achieve the qualification you will not receive a qualification certificate, and the grade will be shown as unclassified.

The marks of each assessment will be converted into a percentage mark and rounded up or down to the nearest whole number. This percentage mark is then weighted according to the weighting of the unit assessment or synoptic assessment within the qualification. The resulting weighted assessment percentages are combined to arrive at a percentage mark for the whole qualification.

Grade definition	Percentage threshold
Distinction	90–100%
Merit	80–89%
Pass	70–79%
Unclassified	0–69% Or failure to pass one or more assessment/s

Re-sits

Some AAT qualifications such as the AAT Advanced Diploma in Accounting have restrictions in place for how many times you are able to re-sit assessments. Please refer to the AAT website for further details.

You should only be entered for an assessment when you are well prepared and you expect to pass the assessment.

AAT qualifications

The material in this book may support the following AAT qualifications:

AAT Advanced Diploma in Accounting Level 3, AAT Advanced Diploma in Accounting at SCQF Level 6 and Further Education and Training Certificate: Accounting Technician (Level 4 AATSA).

Supplements

From time to time we may need to publish supplementary materials to one of our titles. This can be for a variety of reasons. From a small change in the AAT unit guidance to new legislation coming into effect between editions.

You should check our supplements page regularly for anything that may affect your learning materials. All supplements are available free of charge on our supplements page on our website at:

www.bpp.com/learning-media/about/students

Improving material and removing errors

There is a constant need to update and enhance our study materials in line with both regulatory changes and new insights into the assessments.

From our team of authors BPP appoints a subject expert to update and improve these materials for each new edition.

Their updated draft is subsequently technically checked by another author and from time to time non-technically checked by a proof reader.

We are very keen to remove as many numerical errors and narrative typos as we can but given the volume of detailed information being changed in a short space of time we know that a few errors will sometimes get through our net.

We apologise in advance for any inconvenience that an error might cause. We continue to look for new ways to improve these study materials and would welcome your suggestions. If you have any comments about this book, the BPP author of this edition can be emailed at: learningmedia@bpp.com.

Question Bank

Assessment objective 1 – Ethics for Accountants

Task 1.1

Rajesh is a part qualified accounting technician who has recently become employed by RMS Accountancy, a medium sized firm which provides a variety of bookkeeping and accounting services for local businesses.

Rajesh and Jennifer, another accountant at RMS, have been discussing professional ethics and the ways in which the AAT *Code of Professional Ethics* applies to them. During this discussion Rajesh made the following comments.

(a) **Are these statements true or false?**

Statement	True	False
'I know I act ethically as I have never broken the law and always comply with regulations.'		
'The AAT *Code of Professional Ethics* is legally binding if you are a member of the AAT.'		

One of RMS's clients, Carmichael Ltd, has been allocated to Rajesh. Carmichael Ltd is owned by Rajesh's sister, Manju.

(b) **This situation represents which one of the following threats to Rajesh's compliance with the fundamental principles?**

	✓
Familiarity	
Self-interest	
Advocacy	

(c) **If Rajesh carries out this work, which fundamental principle would he be most at risk of breaching?**

	✓
Integrity	
Objectivity	
Confidentiality	

(d) **Which is the most appropriate action for Rajesh to take?**

Action	✓
Resign from RMS Accountancy	
Inform RMS Accountancy of his link with Carmichael Ltd	
Inform the AAT of his link with Carmichael Ltd	

RMS Accountancy prides itself on its strong ethical culture which can, in part, be attributed to the 'tone-at-the-top'.

(e) **Which of the below statements best describes what is meant by the tone-at-the-top?**

	✓
Leaders of the firm have issued clear policies on the ethical behaviour expected at RMS Accountancy.	
Leaders of the firm demonstrate the importance of compliance with the fundamental principles.	
Leaders of the firm require that any potential threat to the fundamental principles is communicated to them in order for the most appropriate action to be taken.	

The Institute of Business Ethics (IBE) has set out simple ethical tests for business decisions. It claims that an understanding of the transparency, effect and fairness of the decision can help to assess whether or not it is ethical.

(f) **Complete the following statement.**

[_____ ▼] can be assessed by considering whether or not the decision maker would mind other people knowing the decision that they have taken.

Picklist:

Effect
Fairness
Transparency

The AAT *Code of Professional Ethics* identifies safeguards for members in practice which can be used in the work environment to protect against threats to the fundamental principles.

(g) **Are these statements about safeguards true or false?**

Statement	True	False
Disciplinary procedures are an example of a safeguard.		
Safeguards always eliminate threats of unethical behaviour from the organisation.		
Undertaking continuing professional development is considered to be one safeguarding measure.		
The AAT *Code of Professional Ethics* makes the recommendation for breaches of ethical requirements to be reported.		
AAT only accept complaints of unethical behaviour from employers or members of the public.		

(h) Charlotte Brown is an accountant in practice, working in a small firm of accountants. She has discovered that a client has been fraudulently selling counterfeit goods and money laundering the proceeds of these sales.

Complete the following statement.

Charlotte should disclose confidential information on this matter directly to

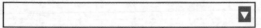

Picklist:

the firm's nominated officer.
the National Crime Agency.
HM Revenue & Customs.
the Conduct Committee.

Task 1.2

(a) Are the following statements regarding professional ethics and the ethical responsibilities of accountants true or false?

Statement	True	False
The AAT *Code of Professional Ethics* provides a set of rules to help accountants determine ethical behaviour.		
The accountancy profession has a responsibility to act in the public interest.		

Tony is an AAT member working in practice who provides accounting services to a number of clients. While Tony is on annual leave his colleague, Janis, is carrying out work for one of his clients on his behalf. Janis has found a significant number of errors in the work Tony has carried out for this client. The client has told Janis that he has lost a large contract due to the overstatement of the loan in his financial statements. Upon his return, Tony is surprised by the number of errors found and states they were due to a lack of skill.

(b) If Tony is found to have failed to exercise reasonable care and skill, could he be liable to the client for the following?

Action	Yes/No
Breach of contract	▼
Negligence	▼
Fraud	▼

Picklist:

Yes
No

Betsy is an accountant working in a small business. One of the company's directors, Marie, has reviewed the financial statements compiled by Betsy and has made a number of changes, including removing information on the names of the directors. Betsy does not agree with this action, however, Marie is insistent that these accounts are filed.

(c) **What is the most appropriate course of action for Betsy to take?**

Action	✓
Betsy should file the financial statements as the director has signed them.	
Betsy should report the company director to the National Crime Agency.	
Betsy should raise her concerns internally stating her concerns in an email to the Board of Directors.	

(d) **'The risk of loss resulting from inadequate or failed processes, people and systems or from external events' is a definition of which of the following?**

Operational risk	
Business risk	
Control risk	

Behaving in an ethical manner involves acting appropriately.

(e) **Complete the following statement.**

Behaving ethically means acting with transparency, honesty, fairness and [▼] in dealings with clients, suppliers, colleagues and others.

Picklist:

confidentiality
respect
discretion

Janis has a number of documents she needs to pass to a partner to sign off. When she takes the documents to his office she finds there is a file regarding the troubled financial state of a client's company. Janis is very familiar with the company as it is her husband's employer.

(f) **Complete the following statement.**

This is a potential [▼] threat on behalf of the junior and looking at the partner's file would be a breach of the [▼] principle.

Picklist 1:

advocacy
familiarity
intimidation
self-interest
self-review

Picklist 2:

confidentiality
integrity
objectivity
professional behaviour
professional competence and due care

(g) **Are the below statements true or false?**

Statement	True	False
The principle of confidentiality must always be carefully abided by in all situations.		
In some situations it is entirely plausible that the principle of integrity could be over-ridden as a result of the circumstances.		

Task 1.3

(a) **Which of the following statements best describes why accountants should comply with a professional code of ethics?**

	✓
It is required by law that they do so.	
To maintain public confidence in the profession.	
To prevent dishonest individuals from entering the profession.	

Denys and Maria are student accounting technicians who are employed by a large accounting firm. During a conversation about the relevance of the AAT *Code of Professional Ethics*, Maria makes the following comments.

(b) **Are these statements true or false?**

Statement	True	False
'The AAT *Code of Professional Ethics* does not apply to me yet as I am only a student accounting technician.'		
'Ethical codes provide advice as to how to comply with the law.'		

(c) **If you have an ethical concern at work, usually the most appropriate first course of action would be to raise this with**

[_____ ▼] **or** [_____ ▼] .

Picklist:

employee helpline
the AAT
trusted colleague
your immediate supervisor

The firm is about to take on a new client and Denys is assisting Jane, a more senior accountant, to carry out due diligence procedures.

Denys asks Jane the following questions.

(d) **Select using the picklist whether Jane would be more likely to answer yes or no to each of Denys' questions.**

Action	
Are customer due diligence procedures only required for new clients?	▼
Is it always acceptable for accountants to pay a referral fee to obtain a new client?	▼
Is it acceptable to offer a commission to employees for bringing in a new client?	▼

Picklist:

Yes
No

In order to help prevent and identify money laundering and terrorist financing, financial institutions and non-financial businesses and professions are required to adopt specific measures. One of these measures is to implement customer due diligence.

(e) **How long should such customer due diligence information be retained?**

	✓
5 years	
7 years	
Indefinitely	

Whistleblowing is the disclosure by an employee of illegal or unethical practices by his or her employer.

(f) **Are these statements relating to whistleblowing true or false?**

Statement	True	False
Whistleblowing should occur as soon as illegal activity is suspected.		
Employees are protected under the Public Information Disclosure Act to ensure they cannot be dismissed for whistleblowing.		
If the disclosure is in the public interest, then the fundamental principle of confidentiality is not breached.		
If the employee is bound by a confidentiality clause in their contract, or has signed a non-disclosure agreement, then the employee could still face dismissal.		

Task 1.4

(a) Complete the following statement.

The UK accountancy profession as a whole is regulated by the

[▼] and global ethical standards are set by the

[▼] .

Picklist:

AAT
CCAB
FRC
IESBA

All professional accountants have a duty to comply with the five fundamental principles.

(b) Are these statements true or false?

Statement	True	False
The duty to comply with the fundamental principles is more relevant to accountants working in practice than accountants working in business.		
Compliance with the law, as well as the policies and procedures of the organisation for which you work will ensure that you never break the five fundamental principles.		

Sharon, an AAT member, is preparing the accounts for a client who has employed her services for a number of years. The client has had a difficult year and will struggle to survive if it cannot secure new finance from a potential investor. The client has asked Sharon to omit details of a number of loans they have taken out during the year. Sharon knows that if she does not do as the client asks, it is likely that they will lose the investor and risk going out of business completely.

(c) This situation is most likely to represent which of the following threats to Sharon's compliance with the fundamental principles?

	✓
Familiarity	
Self-interest	
Intimidation	

(d) **Which of the fundamental principles is threatened?**

	✓
Integrity	
Professional competence and due care	
Confidentiality	

Sharon does not agree to the clients request as she feels this would be a breach of her ethical duty as an accountant.

However, when she presents the accounts to her line manager, Andrew, for review he also suggests that she changes the accounts. Andrew is aware that the firm as a whole is reliant on the client for its own survival and, were this client to go out of business, it is likely that their accountancy business would do. He quietly suggests to Sharon that, if the accounts remain as they are, it is likely that it would not be long before they were both out of a job.

(e) **Select which additional threats to fundamental principles may now also arise.**

Action	✓
Familiarity	
Self-interest	
Intimidation	
Self-review	

(f) **Which of the following actions would be the most appropriate for Sharon to take next?**

	✓
Change the accounts as requested	
Refuse and explain her reasons for doing so with Andrew	
Refuse and inform the media as it is in the public interest to disclose the matter	

Task 1.5

(a) **Are these statements true or false?**

Statement	True	False
Under the AAT *Code of Professional Ethics*, as a minimum you are expected to comply with the laws and regulations of the country in which you live and work.		
The ethical code exists primarily to enhance the public image of accountancy and increase public confidence in the profession.		

(b) **Which of the following best describes what is meant by 'independence'?**

	✓
Ensuring all work is carried out in the public interest	
Having no previous or current links, financial or otherwise, with a client	
Carrying out work objectively and with integrity	

(c) **Rotating senior assurance team personnel helps ensure compliance with the five fundamental principles by safeguarding against which of the following threats?**

	✓
Self-review	
Self-interest	
Familiarity	

13

Marcia is an AAT member who is carrying out an audit of BigBreak Ltd (BB), a holiday company specialising in weekend breaks. During the engagement, Marcia celebrates her 30th birthday and is given an all-inclusive luxury spa break as a birthday gift from the client.

(d) **Which of the below statements best describe the action that Marcia should take?**

	✓
She should accept the gift as it is insignificant and will not influence her audit.	
She should reject the gift as it may appear to others to compromise her objectivity.	
She should reject the gift as it may appear to others to compromise her integrity.	

(e) **Complete the following statement.**

Accountants [▼] accept significant gifts or preferential treatment from a client. This is because it represents [▼] to the fundamental principles.

Picklist:

a familiarity threat
a self-interest threat
no threat
should
should not

The fees paid to accountants by a client for undertaking an assurance engagement could be based on a number of factors.

(f) **Show which of the below could be taken into account when determining fees.**

Action		
The skills required to carry out the engagement		▼
The outcome of the engagement		▼
The value of the service to the client		▼

Picklist:

Could be taken into account
Must not be taken into account

(g)   Are these statements true or false?

Statement	True	False
Tipping off is an offence which may be carried out by accountants.		
Accountants can go to jail if they are found guilty of having been involved in money laundering.		

Task 1.6

(a)   Show whether the below statements are true or false.

Statement	True	False
There are no disadvantages to professional accountants of complying with the AAT *Code of Professional Ethics*.		
Accountants are required under the AAT *Code of Professional Ethics* to comply with all relevant laws and regulations.		
Accountants are required to uphold the reputation of the accounting profession in both their professional and private lives.		

The Institute of Business Ethics (IBE) encourages high standards of ethical behaviour in businesses and it sets out simple ethical tests for a business decision.

(b)   Putting yourself in the place of the people on the receiving end of the decision you are about to make helps you to assess which one of the following?

	✓
Transparency	
Effect	
Fairness	

(c)   In which of the following situations would an accountant be required to breach the fundamental principle of objectivity?

	✓
When it is in the public interest to do so	
When it is required by law to do so	
An accountant should never breach the objectivity principle	

Johnson is a trainee accountant who is applying for a job in a new company that will represent a significant step up in his career. He really wants the job and to help his case he exaggerates the extent of his experience to better suit the expectations set out in the job specification.

(d) **Which ONE of the below statements best describes this situation?**

	✓
Johnson has not compromised his professional ethics; everyone embellishes a little to get a job.	
Johnson has acted irresponsibly and has therefore breached the professional ethic of self-interest.	
Johnson has misled a potential employer and has therefore breached the professional ethic of integrity.	
Johnson has misled a potential employer and has therefore breached the professional ethic of confidentiality.	

Johnson's new employer is a direct competitor of his former employer. When Johnson starts his new job he uses the skills, knowledge and experience that he gained from working for the competitor.

(e) **Show whether the below statements are true or false.**

Statement	True	False
It is fine for Johnson to use these skills, knowledge and experience as the new firm would expect a degree of insider knowledge to be obtained as a perk of employing a former employee of the competition.		
It is fine for Johnson to use these skills, knowledge and experience provided he does not disclose any confidential information.		
It is fine for Johnson to use these skills, knowledge and experience, but only after a reasonable amount of time has elapsed to prevent conflicts of interest arising.		

Professional accountants must maintain the confidentiality of information and not to disclose anything without proper authority.

(f) Show whether the below statements are true or false in relation to the above.

Statement	True	False
This is an ethical principle.		
This is a legal obligation.		

Task 1.7

(a) Business ethics suggest that businesses have a duty to act in the best interests of which of the following?

	✓
The shareholders or other key investors	
The employees of the organisation	
Society as a whole (including shareholders and employees)	

(b) In which of the following situations would an accountant be required to breach confidentiality? Choose all that apply.

	✓
Providing working papers to a new firm who is taking on a former client	
As a result of an enquiry by AAT	
To a financial institution who has requested the information directly from your firm of accountants	
To protect a member's professional interest in a court of law	

(c) Which of the following statements best describe what is meant by 'tone-at-the-top'?

	✓
Senior management set clear policies and procedures that are cascaded down through the organisation.	
Senior management lead by example.	
Senior management establish a clear disciplinary procedure to ensure ethical breaches are escalated to be dealt with at the top of the organisation.	

Rita has discovered that she may have been involved in a money laundering operation without her knowledge. She is worried that she may be incriminated if she reports the issue and is fearful of losing her job and damaging her reputation. The money laundering scheme was very small scale and so Rita makes the decision not to disclose the matter. She confronts the perpetrator and informs them that she will have no further dealings with them.

(d)   Could Rita be guilty of money laundering?

	✓
No, she was unaware of being involved in money laundering and withdrew from the engagement as soon as she suspected wrong doing.	
No, the money laundering scheme was very small scale and would therefore be below the threshold for criminal conviction.	
Yes, if she has been part of the scheme, even unknowingly, she could still be guilty of money laundering.	

(e)   Show whether the below statements are true or false.

Statement	True	False
Rita has tipped off the client.		
If Rita does fail to disclose her suspicions of money laundering she may face additional charges.		
If Rita was to make a protected disclosure she may have a defence against any money laundering charges brought against her.		
If Rita was to make an authorised disclosure she may have a defence against any money laundering charges brought against her.		

(f)   Complete the following sentence.

When unethical or illegal behaviour is uncovered, whistleblowing should be carried out [＿＿＿＿ ▼]. External whistleblowing should take place [＿＿＿＿ ▼] internal discussion with management.

Picklist:

as a last resort
following
immediately
prior to
rather than

Task 1.8

(a) **Complete the following sentence.**

The AAT requires its members to behave in a way that maintains its reputation, maintains [▼] and protects the [▼] .

Picklist:

best interests of the industry
future of the industry
public confidence
public interest
superior quality of output
users of accounting information

Raffaella is being investigated by the AAT for misconduct as a result of failing to complete the CPD requirements expected of her. She has also failed to reply to an item of correspondence from the AAT.

(b) **Do Raffaella's actions represent conclusive proof of misconduct?**

Action	Yes/No
Failing to comply with the AAT's CPD requirements	▼
Failing to reply to an item of correspondence from the AAT	▼

Economic, social and environmental responsibilities of finance professionals are interlinked and is sometimes referred to as a 'triple bottom line' approach.

(c) **Using the picklist below show whether the following suggestions help to address the economic, social or environmental responsibilities of finance professionals.**

Action	Economic/Social/Environmental
Carrying out a conference call between various members of regional staff	▼
Holding an away day for members of the finance department	▼
Reducing the future cost of electricity by investing in solar panels	▼

Christie is a professional accountant in practice who has had Alpha Ltd as a client for many years. In her professional capacity, Christie has been asked by Alpha Ltd's new landlord to give a written reference confirming that the company is likely to be able to pay rent over the next five years. Alpha Ltd is paying a large fee for supplying the reference.

(d)   Show whether the below statements are true or false.

Statement	True	False
Christie should not accept this engagement as the large fee compromises her integrity.		
It would be acceptable practice for Christie to include a disclaimer or liability in the written reference.		
Christie should not accept this engagement as the length of the relationship with the client compromises her objectivity.		
Christie should not accept this engagement as a safeguard against the threat of intimidation presented by this situation.		

(e)   Complete the following sentence.

If Christie gives the reference, even though she knows that Alpha limited has no means of paying the rent, she would be committing [▼] .

Picklist:

fraud by breach of position
fraud by failing to disclose information
fraud by false representation

(f) **Are the following statements relating to taxation services true or false?**

Statement	True	False
When a member in practice submits a tax return on behalf of a client the responsibilities of the member should be made clear in a letter of engagement.		
When a member in practice submits a tax return on behalf of the client, the member assumes all responsibility for the return and computations.		

Task 1.9

(a) Threats to professional competence and due care may be safeguarded by continuing professional development (CPD).

Can CPD also help to safeguard against threats to the following fundamental principles?

Fundamental principle	Yes	No
Confidentiality		
Integrity		

There are certain services that an accountant cannot legally offer unless they are authorised to do so by the relevant regulatory body in the UK. These services are known as 'reserved areas'.

(b) **Which of the following services are considered to be reserved areas?**

Action	✓
Internal auditing	
Insolvency practice	
Taxation services	

(c) **'Meeting the needs of the present without compromising the ability of future generations to meet their own needs' is the definition of which of the following?**

	✓
Corporate Social Reporting (CSR)	
Ethical business practices	
Sustainability	

You are an accountant working in practice and have, for several years, carried out work for two competing hairdressing businesses, Hair By Me and Hair to Infinity. A lease has just become available on the high street in the town in which the two businesses operate. It is in a highly desirable location and both businesses are keen to take on the lease. They have both asked you to act for them in relation to the bid for the lease. On discovery that they were both bidding for the same lease both hairdressing businesses have, independently, offered you an additional £4,000 to act for them exclusively. Neither business is willing for you to act for both parties with respect to the lease.

(d) **Select which of the following fundamental principles are threatened by the above situation.**

Action	✓
Integrity	
Objectivity	
Confidentiality	
Professional competence and due care	
Professional behaviour	

The AAT *Code of Professional Ethics* provides general principles for ethical issues relating to taxation.

(e) Complete the following statement

The AAT *Code of Professional Ethics* says that 'a member providing professional tax services has a duty to put forward the best position in favour of [▼] .'

Picklist:

a client or employer
the public
the tax authorities

Rakhee, an AAT member working in the charity sector, has taken on a new member of staff, Mo. Mo is frequently on the phone during normal working hours and sometimes disappears from his desk for long periods of time to make extended personal calls.

(f) What is the most appropriate action for Rakhee to take?

	✓
Escalate the matter to her line manager	
Report Mo to the AAT	
Discuss the situation with Mo and encourage him to make his phone calls outside normal working hours	

Task 1.10

(a) Overall responsibility for ethics in the accountancy profession rests with which of the following organisations?

	✓
IFAC	
IESBA	
CCAB	

A report by the Nolan Committee established *The Seven Principles of Public Life*. These are the principles we would expect holders of public office to take into consideration in their actions in public life.

(b) **Which TWO of the following are set out by the Nolan Committee in the *Seven Principles of Public Life*?**

	✓
Honesty	
Confidentiality	
Accountability	
Discretion	

The fundamental principle of professional competence and due care requires accountants to only undertake work in which they have suitable skills and experience in order to be able to complete.

(c) **Which of the following types of legal action could be faced by an accountant who fails to act with sufficient expertise? Select all that apply.**

Action	✓
Breach of contract	
Breach of trust	
Professional negligence	
Fraud accusations	

Lana is a self-employed accountant who specialises in carrying out bookkeeping and accountancy work for other small businesses. She has become aware that one of her clients, a self-employed electrician has been offering clients a lower rate for cash payment. The electrician is not VAT registered, but you suspect that he may be working for cash in order to avoid declaring this income on his tax return.

(d)   Which of the following actions would be most appropriate for Lana to take?

	✓
Report the electrician to his trade regulatory body	
Cease to work on behalf of the electrician	
Disclose the matter publicly as the matter is one of public interest	

Alfred is a professional accountant working in practice. He has begun to suspect one of his clients, François, of money laundering.

(e)   Select which of the following statements are true or false.

Statement	True	False
If Alfred does not disclose his suspicions of money laundering, then he himself will have committed a criminal offense.		
Failure to disclose money laundering suspicions can result in a fine up to £10,000.		
Alfred must ensure that he makes François aware that the relevant disclosures have been made.		

(f)   Which ONE of the following disclosures should Alfred make in this scenario?

	✓
Protected disclosure	
Authorised disclosure	
Anonymous disclosure	

Task 1.11

(a) **Which of the following statements relating to the threat of advocacy are true or false?**

Statement	True	False
An accountant who is employed by an organisation is more likely to face an advocacy threat than an accountant working in practice.		
A dominant individual attempting to influence your decisions is an example of a threat of advocacy.		
The fundamental principle most likely to be compromised as the result of an advocacy threat is objectivity.		

Hannah is working on an audit engagement for a client. She is struggling to complete the work in the amount of time available and is finding that she is having to work very long days in an attempt to finish the engagement on time.

(b) **Which of Hannah's fundamental principles listed below could this compromise?**

	✓
Professional behaviour	
Professional competence and due care	
Integrity	

(c) **Using the picklist below, show whether the following offences would be prosecuted in a criminal court or heard in a civil court.**

Action		
Misappropriation of assets		▼
Money laundering		▼
Negligence		▼
Fraud		▼

Picklist:

Civil
Criminal

After the loss of several client records, ABC company brought in an IT consultant who proved that ABS company has recently had their computer system hacked.

(d) Which of the following types of operational risk is presented by the above situation?

	✓
Internal fraud	
External fraud	
Systems failure	

Lucy has just finished an audit engagement for an events management company and has issued an unqualified report. She enjoyed the time spent with the client, in particular discussing her shared love of music festivals with some of the key staff.

At the end of the engagement, Lucy finds the following message in her inbox.

Hi Lucy,

Hope that you are well.

Thank you for your hard work in auditing our accounts and issuing an unqualified report. The whole team is really happy with the result and we would like to offer you two tickets to the sold out Magic Fields festival along with backstage passes so you can meet your favourite band.

(e) Which of the following actions should Lucy now take?

	✓
Go to the festival, it is a once in a lifetime opportunity and she knows that she carried out her work in accordance with the AAT *Code of Professional Ethics*	
Inform her manager that the offer has been made to her	
Refuse the tickets and report the matter to AAT	

Peter is an accountant working in practice. He has just realised that he is caught up in a client's money laundering activities. He panics and shreds the evidence in his client's files.

(f) **Select whether the following statements are true or false in this scenario.**

Action	True	False
Peter could be found guilty of money laundering.		
Peter could be found guilty of the offense of tipping off.		
Peter could be found guilty of prejudicing the investigation.		

Assessment objective 2 – Ethics for accountants/Advanced Bookkeeping/Final Accounts Preparation

Task 2.1

Liz Turner has been trading for just over 12 months as a dressmaker. She has kept no accounting records at all, and she is worried that she may need professional help to sort out her financial position, and she has approached you.

You meet with Liz and discuss the information that you require her to give you. Sometime later, you receive a letter from Liz providing you with the information that you requested, as follows:

(i) She started her business on 1 October 20X7. She opened a business bank account and paid in £8,000 of her savings.

(ii) During October she bought the equipment and the inventory of materials that she needed. The equipment cost £3,800. All of this was paid for out of the business bank account.

(iii) A summary of the business bank account for the twelve months ended 30 September 20X8 showed the following.

Bank statement extract

	£		£
Capital	8,000	Equipment	3,800
Cash banked from sales	32,000	Purchases of materials	20,750
		General expenses	400
		Drawings	14,370
		Balance c/d	680
	40,000		40,000

(iv) All of the sales are on a cash basis. Some of the cash is paid into the bank account while the rest is used for cash expenses. She has no idea what the total value of her sales is for the year, but she knows that she has spent an additional £3,200 in cash on materials and an additional £490 in cash on general expenses. She took the rest of the cash not banked for her private drawings. She also keeps a cash float of £100.

(v)   The gross profit margin on all sales is 50%.

(vi)   Total purchases for the year are £25,550 and total cost of sales for the year is £24,350.

You are required to:

(a)   Calculate the sales for the year ended 30 September 20X8.

£ [   ]

(b)   Show the entries that would appear in Liz Turner's cash account. Use the picklist provided to select the correct account name.

Cash account

Account		£	Account		£
▼			▼		
▼			▼		
▼			▼		
▼			▼		
▼			▼		
Total			Total		

Picklist:

Balance c/d (float)
Bank account
Capital
Drawings
General expenses
Purchases of materials
Sales

(c)   Calculate the total drawings made by Liz Turner throughout the year.

£ [   ]

(d) Select the **TWO** principles from the list below which are outlined in the **AAT** *Code of Professional Ethics.*

	✓
Integrity	
Selflessness	
Honesty	
Objectivity	

(e) Which **THREE** of the following statements reflect the purpose behind the **AAT** *Code of Professional Ethics*?

	✓
Maintain the reputation of the accountancy profession	
Increase opportunities for AAT members	
Act in the public interest	
Ensure protection from negligence claims	
Ensure professional knowledge and skill of AAT members and students	

Task 2.2

You are preparing the year end accounting records for Thomas Brand, who is a sole trader and has a plumbing business.

Thomas' friend, Bill Bailey, did a few months of an accountancy course and decided he would be able to do Thomas' accounts for him. However, Bill has decided that the business is too complex, so Thomas has brought the accounts to Blithe & Co Accountants.

Bill has drafted a trial balance as at 31 December 20X9. However, you discover a number of items which need to be recorded in the accounts.

Account	Debit £	Credit £
Bank	22,450	
Capital		13,200
Purchase ledger control account		4,095
Sales ledger control account	6,725	
Sales		45,200
Purchases	32,570	
Administration costs	750	
	62,495	62,495

A number of items require your attention

- A new vehicle has been acquired for £16,200. It is expected to be sold after five years for £3,800. Vehicles will be depreciated on a straight line basis, with a full year's depreciation in the year of acquisition.

- Sales for December of £1,700 have not yet been recorded. The customer had not paid his invoice at year end.

- A customer paid his outstanding invoice of £800 on 31 December, and this has not yet been recorded.

- Drawings of £1,600 have not yet been recorded in the accounts.

(a) Calculate the depreciation charge for the year on the new vehicle.

£ [ ]

(b) Complete the journal entries using the picklist below, for the acquisition of the new vehicle.

Details	£	Debit ✓	Credit ✓
▼			
▼			

Picklist:

Accumulated depreciation
Bank
Depreciation expense
Purchase ledger control account
Sales ledger control account
Vehicle cost

(c) **Complete the journal entry, using the picklist below, for the depreciation charge on the new vehicle.**

Details	£	Debit ✓	Credit ✓
▼			
▼			

Picklist:

Accumulated depreciation
Bank
Depreciation expense
Purchase ledger control account
Sales ledger control account
Vehicle cost

(d) **Complete the extended trial balance below, including your information calculated in parts (b) and (c) and the missing information in the narrative in respect of sales, drawings and trade receivables. Calculate the totals at the bottom of the debit and credit columns in your final trial balance.**

Account	Ledger balance Debit £	Ledger balance Credit £	Adjustments Debit £	Adjustments Credit £	Trial balance Debit £	Trial balance Credit £
Bank	22,450					
Capital		13,200				
Purchase ledger control account		4,095				
Sales ledger control account	6,725					
Sales		45,200				

Account	Ledger balance Debit £	Ledger balance Credit £	Adjustments Debit £	Adjustments Credit £	Trial balance Debit £	Trial balance Credit £
Purchases	32,570					
Administration costs	750					
Drawings						
Vehicles – Cost						
Vehicles Accumulated depreciation						
Depreciation expense						
Totals	62,495	62,495				

Task 2.3

Wahleed Mansoor is a sole trader who manufacturers skateboards. The following information has been provided about events on the last day of the year:

- Minor Limited, a customer with a receivable outstanding of £950 has gone into liquidation. It is not expected that this debt will be recoverable.

- A new machine is purchased for £5,000. It will have a useful life of 5 years, and a full year of depreciation is charged in the first year of acquisition. The purchase of the machine has been entered into the trial balance, however, the depreciation has not yet been calculated.

(a) **Prepare the journal using the picklist provided for the irrecoverable debts adjustment against the debt of Minor Limited.**

Details		Debit £	Credit £
	▼		
	▼		

34

Picklist:

Bank

Irrecoverable debt expense

Sales ledger control account

(b) Calculate the depreciation charge for the year ended 31 December 20X8.

£ [   ]

(c) Prepare the journal for the depreciation charge as calculated in part (b). Use the picklist provided.

Details		Debit £	Credit £
	▼		
	▼		

Picklist:

Accumulated depreciation

Depreciation expense

(d) List the FOUR enhancing qualitative characteristics as laid out in the *Conceptual Framework*.

[   ]

Wahleed has been trying to clear an unknown balance on his trial balance. He knows he needs to look at the following transactions, but is at a loss as how to clear the balance on the suspense account. The following information is provided:

- A stationery invoice of £1,450 was correctly posted to the bank account, however, it was posted to the office expenses account as £1,540.

- Drawings of £750 had been reflected in the bank and cash account only.

- Rent payment of £900 was posted as a credit to the rent account and a debit to the bank.

(e) **Using the information provided, complete the suspense account and clear the outstanding balance for Wahleed.**

Suspense account

Details	£	Details	£
Balance b/d	660	▼	
▼		▼	
Total		Total	

Picklist:

Balance c/d
Bank
Drawings
Office expenses
Rent accrual
Rent expense

....

Task 2.4

Bella Parker is a sole trader who sells wooden toys. She has drawn up her trial balance at the end of the year 31 December 20X7.

	Debit £	Credit £
Revenue		195,500
Purchases	143,250	
Opening inventory	10,000	
Closing inventory	13,500	13,500
Office expenses	750	
Insurance	1,400	
Drawings	24,000	
Trade receivable	1,200	
Trade payable		1,350
Accruals		3,200
Prepayments	900	

	Debit £	Credit £
Capital		70,000
Cash at bank	86,050	
Suspense	2,500	
	283,550	283,550

The following items were noted:

- Drawings of £2,000 were correctly credited to the bank account, however, no entry was made on the drawings account.

- Cash sales of £500 were banked, however, Bella forgot to include them in the sales account.

- An insurance invoice was posted correctly to the trade payables account, however, the entry was then credited to the insurance account. The invoice was for £500.

- A van was purchased for £8,000 on the last day of the year. It is expected to last 5 years after which it will be sold for scrap for £500. A full year's depreciation will be charged in the year of acquisition.

(a) **Using the information in the narrative above, show the correcting entries in the suspense account below which clear the account.**

Suspense account

Details		£	Details		£
▼			▼		
▼			▼		
			▼		

Picklist:

Balance b/d
Balance c/d
Drawings
Insurance
Sales

(b) **Calculate the depreciation charge for the van.**

£ [   ]

(c) **Enter the adjustments into the extended trial balance below, showing the revised figures for the draft financial statements.**

	Initial trial balance		Adjustments		Revised trial balance	
	Debit £	Credit £	Debit £	Credit £	Debit £	Credit £
Sales		195,500				
Purchases	143,250					
Opening inventory	10,000					
Closing inventory	13,500	13,500				
Office expenses	750					
Insurance	1,400					
Drawings	24,000					
Trade receivable	1,200					
Trade payable		1,350				
Accruals		3,200				
Prepayments	900					
Capital		70,000				
Cash at bank	86,050					
Suspense	2,500					
Motor vehicle						
Depreciation expense						
Accumulated depreciation						
	283,550	283,550				

(d) **Calculate the gross profit of Bella's business for the year ended 31 December 20X7.**

£ [   ]

....

Assessment objective 3 – Advanced Bookkeeping/Final Accounts Preparation/ Management Accounting: Costing

Task 3.1

Green Bean Limited is a business which makes ready meals for sale to supermarkets. It has several large non-current assets in its factory, and needs some assistance in accounting for some adjustments during the financial year ending 31 December 20X8.

Company policy is to charge a full year's depreciation charge in the year of acquisition and none in the year of disposal.

The following details have been extracted from the non-current asset ledger as at 1 January 20X8.

	Cost	Accumulated depreciation	Carrying amount
Aygosh 100	120,000	20,000	100,000
Masher A	85,000	70,000	15,000
Scrawler B	45,000	20,000	25,000

The following additional information is available

- The Masher A was disposed of on the 1 December 20X8. It was sold for £20,000.

- Depreciation has not yet been calculated for the year ended 31 December 20X8, These assets are depreciated on a diminishing balance basis at 25%.

(a) Calculate the depreciation expense for the year ended 31 December 20X8.

£

(b) **Complete the following journal to account for the disposal of the Masher A asset.**

	Debit £	Credit £
Bank and cash		
Non-current assets – cost		
Non-current asset – accumulated depreciation		
Profit and loss account		

Green Bean plans to invest in a new piece of machinery to replace Masher A. There are two options: the Boggler 25 and the Gruncher 30. Green Bean uses a discount rate of 6% to calculate net present value.

The Boggler 25 would cost £68,000 and its net present value has been calculated as £17,360 over its useful life of 5 years.

The Gruncher 30 would cost £105,000. The net present value still needs to be calculated.

(c) **Calculate the net present value of the Gruncher 30 cashflows, rounding to the nearest whole pound where necessary.**

Year	Cash flow £	Discount factor 6%	Discounted cash flow £
0	(105,000)	1.000	
1	43,400	0.943	
2	52,300	0.890	
3	54,800	0.840	

(d) **Discuss which machine would be a better investment.**

Task 3.2

Jemima works as an accounts assistant in a mid-sized accountancy firm. Jemima has received some financial information from one of the clients, Peter Lapin, a sole trader, who only started to trade recently.

- All of Peter's sales are on a cash basis with no customers receiving any credit terms. He receives credit terms from his suppliers.
- Sales are calculated at a 25% gross mark up.
- Here is an incomplete cash at bank extract which Peter has pulled together for Jemima.

Cash at bank

Account	£	Account	£
Balance b/d	10,000	Motor expenses	650
Receipts from customers	36,000		
		Payments to suppliers	25,000
		Balance c/d	14,850
Total		Total	

(a) **Calculate the drawings (assuming all transactions go through the bank account) for Peter Lapin.**

£	

(b) **Calculate the cost of sales figure for Peter's business using the information provided. You must show your workings.**

This is Peter's first year of trading. He has made two purchases of inventory over the year ended 31 March 20X7:

- 1 April 20X6 – purchased 4,000 units at £12 per unit
- 1 October 20X6 – purchased 6,500 units at £12.50 per unit.

Peter has sold 2,500 units each quarter at £20 per unit.

(c) **Calculate the cost of closing inventory using the FIFO method. You must show your workings.**

(d) **Explain TWO advantages and TWO disadvantages of using the FIFO method to measure inventory cost.**

....

Task 3.3

You are Zahit, the assistant accountant helping to prepare the annual financial statements for SquareGo for the year ended 31 December 20X6.

SquareGo received an invoice for telephone charges on 1 December 20X6. The details of the bill were as follows:

- line rental charge of £1,800 covering the period from 1 December 20X6 to 28 February 20X7

- call charges of £500 for calls made between 1 September 20X6 and 30 November 20X6 at a rate of £0.06 per minute.

The invoice was settled on 28 December 20X6.

(a) **Explain the accrual basis in relation to the telephone invoice.**

(b) Select correct J/E in respect of telephone line rental prepayment.

	Details	Debit £	Credit £
A	Telephone expense	600	
	Prepayment		600
B	Telephone expense	1,200	
	Prepayment		1,200
C	Prepayment	600	
	Telephone expense		600
D	Prepayment	1,200	
	Telephone expense		1,200

(c) Explain what fixed and variable costs are, and classify the costs in the invoice.

Assessment objective 4 – Ethics for Accountants/Final Accounts Preparation

Task 4.1

When a partner joins or leaves a partnership there will be a number of procedures to be made to the partnership accounts. These can include adjustments to amounts in the capital accounts and also a new agreements on the profit share ratio. One adjustment that may be needed is to goodwill.

(a) **Explain what is meant by 'goodwill'.**

(b) **What ethical principle is most at risk with goodwill valuations and suggest a safeguard that could help reduce your chosen risk.**

Maria Lemieux has a business selling sportswear and she currently operates as a sole trader. Maria has asked for your advice outlining the advantages and disadvantages of bringing her best friend, Wendy Gretsky into the business. Wendy has experience of designing sportswear for a large national business.

(c) **Write an email to Maria, explaining the advantages and disadvantages of operating as a partnership. Also comment on any actions to take if she chooses to bring Wendy into the business as a partner.**

To
From
Date
Subject

Task 4.2

Jemima works as an accounts assistant in a mid-sized accountancy firm and her work has so far involved the preparation of financial statements for sole traders. Her supervisor has now requested for Jemima to prepare a set of financial statements for a limited company without any additional training.

(a) **According to the AAT** *Code of Professional Ethics,* **identify the ethical principle that Jemima is most at risk if she undertakes this work.**

(b) **Outline suggested safeguards that Jemima can follow to reduce the risk of breaching this principle.**

(c) **Explain FIVE differences between financial statements preparation for companies and those of sole traders that Jemima should be aware of.**

....

Task 4.3

While producing a set of accounts for a partnership, Tomaz identifies that entertainment expenses have increased by 500% from previous years. On further investigation Tomaz discovers the partnership previously had two people required for expense authorisation; one to raise an expense claim and another to check and authorise the claim. However, now only one individual raises the claim and authorises payment.

(a) **Identify the threats and ethical principles that are most at risk here.**

(b) **What safeguards can be put in place to reduce the risks that Tomaz faces?**

(c) **What are the typical contents of a partnership agreement?**

....

Task 4.4

A large business has set its materiality level at £5,000 and it has been discovered that two purchase invoices have been fraudulently raised and paid to a member of staff. Each invoice was worth £1,000. A colleague has stated as these amounts are well below the materiality threshold level set there is no need to follow this issue up or investigate further.

(a)   What is meant by the term materiality?

(b)   How should you respond to your colleague regarding whether it should be followed up and if so, what steps should be taken?

Amy is an accounting technician and is in the process of preparing a set of accounts for a sole trader, ABC Supplies. While collecting sales revenue information a customer telephones and asks for Amy to email across other customer details of ABC Supplies. He says he wants this information to be more competitive and without it he may have to take his custom elsewhere.

(c)   What ethical principle and threat is most relevant here?

(d)   What should Amy do in these circumstances and identify when Amy may disclose customer information.

· ·

Task 4.5

When preparing a set of final accounts it is important for the preparer to be aware for any potential conflict of interests.

(a)   Explain what is meant by a conflict of interest.

(b)   What is the appropriate procedure for dealing with potential conflicts of interest?

Jaz is an accountant in a large accountancy practice and is the process of preparing the final accounts for two separate clients, A and B. After reviewing a member of her staff's working papers Jaz discovers that client A has made a substantial loan (£1m) to B. Jaz is fully aware that B is facing serious financial difficulties and there are doubts whether B will continue to be a going concern in the foreseeable future.

(c)   What is the threat that Jaz is facing here and what safeguards can Jaz put in place?

· ·

Task 4.6

A business trading as a sole trader or a partnership will be financed by capital invested into the business by its owners and money taken out of the business for the benefit of the owners will be in the form of drawings.

(a) **Looking at capital and drawings explain how this differs from an organisation trading as a limited company.**

An accountant has prepared a limited company set of accounts that has an inflated equity figure effectively overvaluing the company by a considerable amount. This value was used to secure a substantial bank loan. The company has since ceased to trade with the loss of many jobs. After financial press interest in the matter it was found the accountant did not perform the necessary checks to see if this reported equity figure was correct even though equity had increased to £2m from just £25,000 reported in the previous year.

(b) **Identify the two ethical principles that are most at risk here.**

(c) **Explain what is meant by the term professional scepticism.**

Task 4.7

Buildings, machinery, IT equipment and goods purchased for resale are assets which typically have a substantial value in a business. To help reduce the risk of any material misstatement in the final accounts there are two accounting standards that provide guidance on valuation of these types of assets.

Required

(a) **Identify the two accounting standards that provide guidance on the accounting treatment of non-current assets such as buildings and current assets of goods purchases for resale.**

(b) **If an accountant did not keep up to date with changes in accounting standards what ethical principle would be most at risk?**

(c) **How can an accountant keep up to date with changes in the accountancy profession and what are the consequences when skills are not up to date?**

Assessment objective 5 – Management Accounting: Costing

Task 5.1

You are Ian Chesterton, a part-qualified accounting technician. You work for Hammond Co, which manufactures luxury office furniture.

You cover all aspects of bookkeeping and accounting for the business. You report to Tom Howard, Chief Accountant.

Today's date is 3 January 20X0.

The board of Hammond Co is currently considering an investment in new plant and machinery, which will enable the company to sell a more comfortable make of its office chair. The board will make a decision about this next week. The investment will take place immediately afterwards if the board decides to go ahead.

You have been asked to complete an analysis for the board meeting of this investment, using the net present value (NPV) and payback methods of investment appraisal.

- Hammond Co will need to make an immediate investment in plant and machinery of £240,000.

- Expected sales revenue of the new chair in Year 1 will be £200,000 and expected variable costs will be £100,000.

- Sales revenue and costs are expected to rise by the following percentages in Years 2–4 compared with the previous year.

Year	2	3	4
	10%	5%	3%

- Expected fixed costs will be £20,000 per year and will not change over the four year period.

(a) **Complete the following table rounding to the nearest whole pound.**

Year	Year 0 £	Year 1 £	Year 2 £	Year 3 £	Year 4 £
Capital expenditure					
Sales revenue					
Variable costs					
Fixed costs		20,000	20,000	20,000	20,000
Net cash flows					
PV factors	1.000	0.917	0.842	0.772	0.708
Discounted cash flows (to nearest £)					
Net present value					

(b) **Calculate the payback period for the new plant and machinery to the nearest whole month.**

The payback period is [   ] year(s) and [   ] month(s).

Task 5.2

You are Dodo Chaplet, a part-qualified accounting technician. You work for Maxwell Co, a company that manufactures high quality cosmetic creams.

You cover all aspects of bookkeeping and accounting for the business. You report to Kate Harvey, the Head of Accounts.

The budgeted and actual figures for the quarter to 31 March 20X4 are as follows:

	Budget	Actual
Volume sold	40,000	45,000
	£	**£**
Sales revenue	920,000	1,040,000
Direct materials	520,000	562,500
Direct labour	45,000	54,600
Variable overheads	55,000	71,300
Fixed overheads	26,000	30,300

Complete the following table. Show your answers to the nearest whole pound. Adverse variances must be denoted with a minus sign or brackets.

	Original budget £ 40,000 units	Flexed budget £ 45,000 units	Actual results £ 45,000 units	Variances £
Sales revenue	920,000		1,040,000	
Direct materials	520,000		562,500	
Direct labour	45,000		54,600	
Variable overheads	55,000		71,300	
Fixed overheads	26,000		30,300	
Operating profit				

Task 5.3

Istanbul Ltd has two profit centres – Production A and B – and one support cost centre, Administration which supports the two profit centres, spending 55% of its time on Production A and the remainder on Production B.

Istanbul's budgeted overheads for quarter ended 30 April 20X3 are:

	Basis of apportionment	£
Depreciation of property, plant and equipment	PPE carrying amount	190,000
Rent and rates	Floor space	360,000
Power	Floor space	243,000
Indirect labour costs:		
Production supervisors	No. of supervisors	140,000
General administration		463,000
		1,396,000

You have been asked to help with the allocation and apportionment of overheads and have the following information:

Department	Floor Space m2	Number of Supervisors	PPE carrying amount £
Production A	1,600	35	3,560
Production B	1,780	25	2,400
Administration			680
TOTAL	3,380	60	6,640

Complete the following overhead apportionment table. Show your answers to the nearest whole pound. Use minus signs where appropriate.

Budgeted overheads	Basis of apportionment	Production A	Production B	Administration	Total
Depreciation	PPE carrying amount				
Rent and rates	Floor space				
Power	Floor space				
Production supervisors	No. of supervisors				
General administration					
Subtotal					
Reapportion administration (55%/45%)					
Total					

Assessment objective 6 – Advanced Bookkeeping/Final Accounts Preparation

Task 6.1

Mr I Jones needs assistance in the completion of his statement of profit or loss.

He has supplied the following trial balance for the year ended 31 May 20X6.

	£	£
Accruals		350
Bank	23,700	
Capital account		33,200
Closing inventory	9,000	9,000
General expenses	63,800	
Drawings	20,000	
Administration costs	3,900	
IT Equipment depreciation expense	850	
IT Equipment accumulated depreciation		3,400
IT Equipment at cost	8,500	
Opening inventory	7,800	
Prepayments	530	
Purchases	150,800	
Purchase ledger control account		16,170
Sales		280,480
Sales ledger control account	14,720	
VAT		3,000
Wages	42,000	
	345,600	345,600

Required

Prepare the statement of profit or loss for the year ended 31 May 20X6.

Mr I Jones

Statement of profit or loss for the year ended 31 May 20X6

	£	£

Task 6.2

Karen, Jake and Saffron are in partnership. You have the following information about the business.

The financial year ends on 31 August 20X6.

Partners' annual salaries:

Karen – £11,400
Jake – £14,400
Saffron – £9,600

Partners' interest on capital:

Karen – £1,000 per full year
Jake – £1,200 per full year
Saffron – £600 per full year

Profit share:

Karen – 20%
Jake – 65%
Saffron – 15%

Profit during the year ended 31 August 20X6 was £180,000.

The partners have requested your assistance in calculating the profit available for distribution between the partners.

Required

Complete the partnership appropriation account in accordance with the partnership agreement for the year ended 31 August 20X6.

	Karen £	Jake £	Saffron £	Total £
Salaries				
Interest on capital				
Profit available for distribution (20% / 65% / 15%)				

....

Task 6.3

Andrew, Brown and Carter are a partnership (ABC) who design and install kitchens.

You are an Accounting Technician at MSP Accountants (MSP), and have been asked to prepare the partnership accounts for the ABC partnership.

You have the following information about the partnership's business:

- The financial year ends on 31 March.

- Brown and Carter each introduced a further £10,000 capital into the bank account on 1 October 20X6.

- Goodwill was valued at £80,000 on 31 March 20X7.

- There was no interest on drawings.

	Andrew	Brown	Carter
Profit share, for the period	40%	30%	30%
Capital account balances at 1 April 20X6	£40,000	£30,000	£30,000
Current account balances at 1 April 20X6	£1,160 credit	£420 credit	£5,570 credit
Drawings for the year ended 31 March 20X7	£2,500 each month	£38,000	£45,000

The appropriation account for the year ended 31 March 20X7 has already been prepared by the accountant.

Partnership appropriation account for the year ended 31 March 20X7

	Total £
Profit for appropriation	156,000
Salaries:	
Andrew	15,000
Brown	18,000
Carter	24,000
Interest on capital:	
Andrew	2,860
Brown	1,980
Carter	1,980
Profit available for distribution	92,180
Profit shares:	
Andrew	36,872
Brown	27,654
Carter	27,654
Total profit distributed	92,180

(a) **Prepare the current accounts for the partners for the year ended 31 March 20X7. Show clearly the balance carried down. Do NOT use brackets, minus signs or dashes.**

Use the picklist provided to select the appropriate account name.

Current accounts

	Andrew £	Brown £	Carter £		Andrew £	Brown £	Carter £
▼				▼			
▼				▼			
▼				▼			
▼				▼			
Total							

Picklist:

Balance b/d
Balance c/d
Drawings
Goodwill
Interest on capital
Salaries
Share of profit or loss

During your work, you discover an anomaly in the underlying records of ABC. You have reason to suspect that one of the partners is incorrectly recording his expenses.

(b) **Who would usually be the most appropriate first person to raise this with?** [▼] or [▼] .

Picklist:

employee helpline
the AAT
HMRC
your immediate supervisor

A fellow junior colleague asks what the term 'whistleblowing' means.

(c)   Are these statements relating to whistleblowing true or false?

Statement	True	False
Employees are protected under the Public Information Disclosure Act provided that they have acted in good faith and the belief is that the environment is being damaged.		
You should start the whistleblowing process as soon as illegal activity is suspected.		
The fundamental principle of confidentiality is not breached, if the disclosure is in the public interest.		
If the organisation has an ethics committee, this should be approached before getting to the whistleblowing stage.		

Task 6.4

James Doolittle is a sole trader who has prepared the following trial balance for his business.

	Debit £	Credit £
Bank	11,950	
Capital		74,300
Payables		40,800
Receivables	35,450	
Allowance for doubtful debts		3,200
Drawings	19,000	
Fixtures and Fittings	24,500	
Electricity	2,050	
Insurance	2,800	

	Debit £	Credit £
Miscellaneous expenses	1,500	
Motor expenses	3,100	
Motor vehicles at cost	48,000	
Purchases	245,000	
Accumulated depreciation – Fixtures and fittings		8,550
– Motor vehicles		29,800
Rent	3,400	
Sales		344,450
Opening inventory	40,200	
Telephone costs	1,950	
VAT		3,050
Wages	54,750	
Closing inventory	43,500	43,500
Depreciation expense – fixtures and fittings	2,450	
Depreciation expense – motor vehicles	7,800	
Accruals		1,000
Prepayments	1,250	
	548,650	548,650

(a) **Prepare the statement of financial position as at 31 March 20X7 based on the information in the trial balance. Use the picklist provided to select the account names as required.**

	Cost £	Accumulated depreciation £	Carrying amount £
Non-current assets			
▼			
▼			
Current assets			
▼			
▼			
▼			
▼			
Current liabilities			
▼			
▼			
▼			
Net current assets			
Net assets			
Financed by:			
▼			
▼			

	Cost £	Accumulated depreciation £	Carrying amount £
Less:			
▼			

Picklist:

Accruals
Capital
Cash and cash equivalents
Inventory
Depreciation charges
Drawings
Electricity
Fixtures & Fittings
Insurance
Miscellaneous expenses
Motor expenses
Motor vehicles
Prepayments
Profit for the year
Purchases
Rent
Sales
Telephone
Trade payables
Trade receivables
VAT
Wages

(b) **The two fundamental qualitative characteristics of financial information, according to the IASB's *Conceptual Framework* are:**

                     [   ] and [   ]

(c) **Select which ONE of the following statements best explains the term 'going concern'.**

	✓
The effect of transactions being recognised when they occur	
That the business will continue in operation for the foreseeable future	
To ensure similar businesses can be compared to allow for investors to assess them	
To ensure the financial statements have been prepared on time	

Task 6.5

Beth Green is a sole trader who has prepared the following trial balance for her business.

	Debit £	Credit £
Drawings	8,050	
Repairs and maintenance	1,250	
Electricity	1,025	
Insurance	900	
Miscellaneous expenses	750	
Motor expenses	1,550	
Motor vehicles at cost	24,000	
Purchases	122,500	
Rent	1,700	
Revenue		171,800
Opening inventory	20,100	
Telephone costs	975	
Bank		3,964
Capital		10,772
Accruals		1,389

	Debit £	Credit £
Closing inventory	21,750	21,750
Depreciation expense – machinery	1,225	
Depreciation expense – motor vehicles	3,900	
	209,675	209,675

The following information is also available

- A customer with an outstanding invoice of £475 has gone into liquidation. This has not yet been reflected in the TB.

Prepare the statement of profit or loss for the year ended 31 December 20X8.

	£	£
Sales revenue		
Less:		
▼		
▼		
▼		
Cost of goods sold		
Gross profit		
Less:		
▼		
▼		
▼		
▼		
▼		
▼		
▼		
▼		
▼		
Total expenses		
Profit/loss for the year		

Picklist:

Accruals
Bank and cash
Capital
Closing inventory
Depreciation charges
Disposal of non-current asset
Drawings
Electricity
Insurance
Irrecoverable debt expense
Miscellaneous expenses
Motor expenses
Opening inventory
Prepayments
Purchases
Rent
Repairs and maintenance
Sales revenue
Telephone
Trade payables
Trade receivables
VAT

Answer Bank

Assessment objective 1 – Ethics for Accountants

Task 1.1

(a)

Statement	True	False
'I know I act ethically as I have never broken the law and always comply with regulations.'		✓
'The AAT *Code of Professional Ethics* is legally binding if you are a member of the AAT.'		✓

(b)

Familiarity	✓
Self-interest	
Advocacy	

(c)

Integrity	
Objectivity	✓
Confidentiality	

(d)

Action	✓
Resign from RMS Accountancy	
Inform RMS Accountancy of his link with Carmichael Ltd	✓
Inform the AAT of his link with Carmichael Ltd	

BPP
LEARNING MEDIA

(e)

Leaders of the firm have issued clear policies on the ethical behaviour expected at RMS Accountancy.	
Leaders of the firm demonstrate the importance of compliance with the fundamental principles.	✓
Leaders of the firm require that any potential threat to the fundamental principles is communicated to them in order for the most appropriate action to be taken.	

(f) | Transparency | can be assessed by considering whether or not the decision maker would mind other people knowing the decision that they have taken.

(g)

Statement	True	False
Disciplinary procedures are an example of safeguard.	✓	
Safeguards always eliminate threats of unethical behaviour from the organisation.		✓
Undertaking continuing professional development is considered to be one safeguarding measure.	✓	
The AAT *Code of Professional Ethics* makes the recommendation for breaches of ethical requirements to be reported.		✓
AAT only accept complaints of unethical behaviour from employers or members of the public.		✓

Safeguards cannot always eliminate threats of unethical behaviour and breaches of the AAT *Code of Professional Ethics*. Instead, where the threats cannot be fully eliminated, they should be reduced to an acceptable level.

The AAT *Code of Professional Ethics* makes it mandatory for breaches to be reported, it becomes 'an explicitly stated duty' (para. 100.16(ii)).

Complaints can also come from colleagues or any other source (para.100.16(i)).

(h) Charlotte should disclose confidential information on this matter directly to the | firm's nominated officer | .

Even a small firm of accountants must have a nominated officer to deal with money laundering concerns. Employees must report their concerns to their nominated officer in the first instance.

Task 1.2

(a)

Statement	True	False
The AAT *Code of Professional Ethics* provides a set of rules to help accountants determine ethical behaviour.		✓
The accountancy profession has a responsibility to act in the public interest.	✓	

The AAT *Code of Professional Ethics* is not a set of rules, but a framework of principles to guide the ethical conduct of its members.

(b)

Action	Yes/No
Breach of contract	Yes
Negligence	Yes
Fraud	No

If an assignment is not completed with due care then this can result in a breach of contract through professional negligence. This means a failure to act with due skill and care, causing loss to another party and there may be a liability to pay the injured party compensation'. He may be liable to be charged with fraud if it can be proved that he acted with intent to defraud the client, however, the question states that he is surprised by the number of errors, so we can assume that it was unintentional in this case, hence 'no' for fraud.

(c)

Action	✓
Betsy should file the financial statements as the director has signed them.	
Betsy should report the company director to the National Crime Agency.	
Betsy should raise her concerns internally stating her concerns in an email to the Board of Directors.	✓

Considering the appropriate action to take, think of the consequences and what are your obligations? In this case, you have already stated your actions to one director, who has chosen to not take the advice. In this case, there is a Board of Directors who will have joint responsibility for the financial statements, so it would be recommended to ensure that all parties who are responsible for the financial statements should be made aware.

(d)

Operational risk	✓
Business risk	
Control risk	

(e) Behaving ethically means acting with transparency, honesty, fairness and discretion in dealings with clients, suppliers, colleagues and others.

(f) This is a potential self-interest threat on behalf of the junior and looking at the partner's file would be a breach of the confidentiality principle.

(g)

Statement	True	False
The principle of confidentiality must always be carefully abided by in all situations.		✓
In some situations it is entirely plausible that the principle of integrity could be over-ridden as a result of the circumstances.		✓

Task 1.3

(a)

It is required by law that they do so	
To maintain public confidence in the profession	✓
To prevent dishonest individuals from entering the profession	

(b)

	True	False
'The AAT *Code of Professional Ethics* does not apply to me yet as I am only a student accounting technician.'		✓
'Ethical codes provide advice as to how to comply with the law.'	✓	

(c) If you have an ethical concern at work, usually the most appropriate first course of action would be to raise this with ⬚ your immediate ⬚ or ⬚ employee helpline ⬚ .

(d)

Action	
Are customer due diligence procedures only required for new clients?	No
Is it always acceptable for accountants to pay a referral fee to obtain a new client?	No
Is it acceptable to offer a commission to employees for bringing in a new client?	Yes

You may offer commissions to employees for introducing new clients. To clarify the point regarding referral fees, these are only acceptable if the client is aware of the third party being paid for the referral. The third party should be similarly bound by professional ethical standards and should be relied upon to maintain their integrity and professional standards.

(e)

5 years	✓
7 years	
Indefinitely	

(f)

	True	False
Whistleblowing should occur as soon as illegal activity is suspected.		✓
Employees are protected under the Public Information Disclosure Act to ensure they cannot be dismissed for whistleblowing.	✓	
If the disclosure is in the public interest, then the fundamental principle of confidentiality is not breached.	✓	
If the employee is bound by a confidentiality clause in their contract, or has signed a non-disclosure agreement, then the employee could still face dismissal.		✓

Task 1.4

(a) The UK accountancy profession as a whole is regulated by the

FRC
IESBA

and global ethical standards are set by the

(b)

Statement	True	False
The duty to comply with the fundamental principles is more relevant to accountants working in practice than accountants working in business.		✓
Compliance with the law, as well as the policies and procedures of the organisation for which you work will ensure that you never break the five fundamental principles.		✓

(c)

Familiarity	✓
Self-interest	
Intimidation	

(d)

Integrity	✓
Professional competence and due care	
Confidentiality	

(e)

Action	
Familiarity	
Self-interest	✓
Intimidation	✓
Self-review	

(f)

Change the accounts as requested	
Refuse and explain her reasons for doing so with Andrew	✓
Refuse and inform the media as it is in the public interest to disclose the matter	

Task 1.5

(a)

Statement	True	False
Under the AAT *Code of Professional Ethics*, as a minimum you are expected to comply with the laws and regulations of the country in which you live and work.	✓	
The ethical code exists primarily to enhance the public image of accountancy and increase public confidence in the profession.		✓

(b)

Ensuring all work is carried out in the public interest	
Having no previous or current links, financial or otherwise, with a client	
Carrying out work objectively and with integrity	✓

(c)

Self-review	
Self-interest	
Familiarity	✓

(d)

She should accept the gift as it is insignificant and will not influence her audit.	
She should reject the gift as it may appear to others to compromise her objectivity.	✓
She should reject the gift as it may appear to others to compromise her integrity.	

(e) Accountants ⟨ should not ⟩ accept significant gifts or preferential treatment from a client. This is because it represents ⟨ a self-interest threat ⟩ to the fundamental principles.

(f)

Action	
The skills required to carry out the engagement	Could be taken into account
The outcome of the engagement	Must not be taken into account
The value of the service to the client	Could be taken into account

A contingent fee is a fee calculated on a predetermined basis relating to the outcome of a transaction or the result of the work performed. Contingent fees are used widely for certain types of non-assurance engagements, for example debt recovery work. There is a risk that they give rise to threats to compliance with the fundamental principles. Therefore, it would not appropriate for an assurance engagement as in this question.

(g)

Statement	True	False
Tipping off is an offence which may be carried out by accountants.	✓	
Accountants can go to jail if they are found guilty of having been involved in money laundering.	✓	

Task 1.6

(a)

Statement	True	False
There are no disadvantages to professional accountants of complying with the AAT *Code of Professional Ethics*.		✓
Accountants are required under the AAT *Code of Professional Ethics* to comply with all relevant laws and regulations.	✓	
Accountants are required to uphold the reputation of the accounting profession in both their professional and private lives.	✓	

By complying with the AAT *Code of Professional Ethics*, it may mean that the member must resign from an assignment or an employment (para.100.9, AAT *Code of Professional Ethics*). Therefore, there is a risk that in order to comply with the AAT *Code of Professional Ethics*, the accountant may have to lose business (resign from the engagement).

Also, it is stated that 'a client...receives competent professional service based on current developments in practice, legislation and techniques...(a) member shall act diligently and in accordance with applicable technical and professional standards...' (para.100.5). The accountant should ensure they are competent and understand the latest laws and regulations.

(b)

	✓
Transparency	
Effect	
Fairness	✓

(c)

	✓
When it is in the public interest to do so	
When it is required by law to do so	
An accountant should never breach the objectivity principle	✓

Objectivity is not one of the principles that can ever be breached, the other options would be more applicable to breaches of confidentiality.

(d)

	✓
Johnson has not compromised his professional ethics; everyone embellishes a little to get a job.	
Johnson has acted irresponsibly and has therefore breached the professional ethic of self-interest.	
Johnson has misled a potential employer and has therefore breached the professional ethic of integrity.	✓
Johnson has misled a potential employer and has therefore breached the professional ethic of confidentiality.	

He has behaved in an unethical manner by embellishing his CV, so he will have breached at least one of the fundamental principles of the AAT *Code of Professional Ethics*. By fabricating some of the content on his CV he is not behaving in an honest and professional manner and is therefore breaching the principle of integrity.

Self-interest is a threat to the fundamental principles, but not one of the fundamental principles itself.

(e)

Statement	True	False
It is fine for Johnson to use these skills, knowledge and experience as the new firm would expect a degree of insider knowledge to be obtained as a perk of employing a former employee of the competition.		✓
It is fine for Johnson to use these skills, knowledge and experience provided he does not disclose any confidential information.	✓	
It is fine for Johnson to use these skills, knowledge and experience, but only after a reasonable amount of time has elapsed to prevent conflicts of interest arising.		✓

(f)

Statement	True	False
This is an ethical principle.	✓	
This is a legal obligation.	✓	

....

Task 1.7

(a)

	✓
The shareholders or other key investors	
The employees of the organisation	
Society as a whole (including shareholders and employees)	✓

(b)

	✓
Providing working papers to a new firm who is taking on a former client	✓
As a result of an enquiry by AAT	✓
To a financial institution who has requested the information directly to your firm of accountants	
To protect a member's professional interest in a court of law	✓

(c)

	✓
Senior management set clear policies and procedures that are cascaded down through the organisation.	
Senior management lead by example.	✓
Senior management establish a clear disciplinary procedure to ensure ethical breaches are escalated to be dealt with at the top of the organisation.	

(d)

	✓
No, she was unaware of being involved in money laundering and withdrew from the engagement as soon as she suspected wrong doing.	
No, the money laundering scheme was very small scale and would therefore be below the threshold for criminal conviction.	
Yes, if she has been part of the scheme, even unknowingly, she could still be guilty of money laundering.	✓

(e)

Statement	True	False
Rita has tipped off the client.		✓
If Rita does fail to disclose her suspicions of money laundering she may face additional charges.	✓	
If Rita was to make a protected disclosure she may have a defence against any money laundering charges brought against her.		✓
If Rita was to make an authorised disclosure she may have a defence against any money laundering charges brought against her.	✓	

(f) When unethical or illegal behaviour is uncovered, whistleblowing should be carried out as a last resort . External whistleblowing should take place following internal discussion with management.

- -

Task 1.8

(a) The AAT requires its members to behave in a way that maintains its reputation, maintains public confidence and protects the public interest .

(b)

Action	Yes/No
Failing to comply with the AAT's CPD requirements	Yes
Failing to reply to an item of correspondence from the AAT	No

(c)

Action	Economic/Social/Environmental
Carrying out a conference call between various members of regional staff	Economic OR Environmental
Holding an away day for members of the finance department	Social
Reducing the future cost of electricity by investing in solar panels	Economic OR Environmental

Note. Both Economic and Environmental are valid answers for the first and third requirements of this question. Marks would be awarded for either of these choices.

(d)

Statement	True	False
Christie should not accept this engagement as the large fee compromises her integrity.		✓
It would be acceptable practice for Christie to include a disclaimer or liability in the written reference.	✓	
Christie should not accept this engagement as the length of the relationship with the client compromises her objectivity.		✓
Christie should not accept this engagement as a safeguard against the threat of intimidation presented by this situation.		✓

(e) If Christie gives the reference, even though she knows that Alpha limited has no means of paying the rent, she would be committing ⬚ fraud by false representation ⬚.

(f)

Statement	True	False
When a member in practice submits a tax return on behalf of a client the responsibilities of the member should be made clear in a letter of engagement.	✓	
When a member in practice submits a tax return on behalf of the client, the member assumes all responsibility for the return and computations.		✓

Task 1.9

(a)

Fundamental principle	Yes	No
Confidentiality		✓
Integrity	✓	

(b)

Action	✓
Internal auditing	
Insolvency practice	✓
Taxation services	

(c)

	✓
Corporate Social Reporting (CSR)	
Ethical business practices	
Sustainability	✓

(d)

Action	✓
Integrity	
Objectivity	✓
Confidentiality	✓
Professional competence and due care	
Professional behaviour	

(e) The AAT *Code of Professional Ethics* says that 'a member providing professional tax services has a duty to put forward the best position in favour of | a client or employer | . '(para.160.3)

(f)

	✓
Escalate the matter to her line manager	
Report Mo to the AAT	
Discuss the situation with Mo and encourage him to make his phone calls outside normal working hours	✓

....

Task 1.10

(a)

	✓
IFAC	✓
IESBA	
CCAB	

(b)

	✓
Honesty	✓
Confidentiality	
Accountability	✓
Discretion	

(c)

Action	✓
Breach of contract	✓
Breach of trust	✓
Professional negligence	✓
Fraud accusations	✓

(d)

Report the electrician to his trade regulatory body	
Cease to work on behalf of the electrician	✓
Disclose the matter publically as the matter is one of public interest	

(e)

Statement	True	False
If Alfred does not disclose his suspicions of money laundering, then he himself will have committed a criminal offense.	✓	
Failure to disclose money laundering suspicions can result in a fine up to £10,000.		✓
Alfred must ensure that he makes François aware that the relevant disclosures have been made.		✓

(f)

Protected disclosure	✓
Authorised disclosure	
Anonymous disclosure	

Task 1.11

(a)

Statement	True	False
An accountant who is employed by an organisation is more likely to face an advocacy threat than an accountant working in practice.		✓
A dominant individual attempting to influence your decisions is an example of a threat of advocacy.		✓
The fundamental principle most likely to be compromised as the result of an advocacy threat is objectivity.	✓	

(b)

	✓
Professional behaviour	
Professional competence and due care	✓
Integrity	

(c)

Action	
Misappropriation of assets	Criminal
Money laundering	Criminal
Negligence	Civil
Fraud	Criminal

(d)

Internal fraud	
External fraud	✓
Systems failure	

(e)

Go to the festival, it is a once in a lifetime opportunity and she knows that she carried out her work in accordance with the AAT *Code of Professional Ethics.*	
Inform her manager that the offer has been made to her.	✓
Refuse the tickets and report the matter to AAT.	

(f)

Action	True	False
Peter could be found guilty of money laundering.	✓	
Peter could be found guilty of the offense of tipping off.		✓
Peter could be found guilty of prejudicing the investigation.	✓	

Assessment objective 2 – Ethics for Accountants/ Advanced Bookkeeping/Final Accounts Preparation

Task 2.1

(a)

£	48,700

Workings

	£
Cost of sales (from question part (ix)	24,350
Total sales (× 2) (gross profit margin 50%)	48,700

(b)

Cash account

Account	£	Account	£
Sales (from (a))	48,700	Bank account (Cash banked from sales)	32,000
		Purchases of materials (per part iv)	3,200
		General expenses (per part iv)	490
		Drawings (balancing figure)	12,910
		Bal c/d (float) per part iv	100
	48,700		48,700

This is the cash account and therefore will not include items which have been paid through the bank account, such as the purchases through the bank.

(c)

£	27,280

Workings

	£
Bank account	14,370
Cash account (from (d))	12,910
Total drawings	27,280

(d)

	✓
Integrity	✓
Selflessness	
Honesty	
Objectivity	✓

Selflessness is one of the Nolan principles not one of the ethical principles from the AAT *Code of Professional Ethics*. Objectivity is stated in the Code as a member ' shall not allow bias, conflict of interest or undue influence of others to override professional or business judgements' (AAT, 2017: p.9) Integrity is stated in the Code as that a member shall 'be straightforward and honest in all professional and business relationships' (AAT, 2017:p.9). Honesty is therefore included within the principle of integrity but is not a stand alone principle under the *Code of Professional Ethics*.

(e)

	✓
Maintain the reputation of the accountancy profession	✓
Increase opportunities for AAT members	
Act in the public interest	✓
Ensure protection from negligence claims	
Ensure professional knowledge and skill of AAT members and students	✓

BPP
LEARNING MEDIA

The AAT *Code of Professional Ethics* requires its members (including students) to behave in a way that maintains the reputation of professional accountants and the accountancy profession (*Code*, s.150.1) ensures professional knowledge and skill of AAT members and students and ensures they act in a diligent and professional manner (*Code*, s.100.5).

It cannot ensure protection against negligence claims (although if an accountant has followed the principles and the Code, then it will assist and support the accountant).The purpose of the Code is not to increase the opportunities per se, however, by ensuring the professionalism of its members, it will add credibility to the AAT as a whole.

Task 2.2

(a)

£	2,480

Workings: $\dfrac{(16,200 - 3,800)}{5} = 2,480$

(b)

Details	£	Debit ✓	Credit ✓
Vehicle cost	16,200	✓	
Bank	16,200		✓

(c)

Details	£	Debit ✓	Credit ✓
Depreciation expense	2,480	✓	
Accumulated depreciation	2,480		✓

(d)

Account	Ledger balance Debit £	Ledger balance Credit £	Adjustments Debit £	Adjustments Credit £	Trial balance Debit £	Trial balance Credit £
Bank	22,450			17,000	5,450	
Capital		13,200				13,200
Purchase ledger control account		4,095				4,095
Sales ledger control account	6,725		900		7,625	
Sales		45,200		1,700		46,900
Purchases	32,570				32,570	
Administration costs	750				750	
Drawings			1,600		1,600	
Vehicles – Cost			16,200		16,200	
Vehicles Accumulated depreciation				2,480		2,480
Depreciation expense			2,480		2,480	
Totals	62,495	62,495	21,180	21,180	66,675	66,675

Task 2.3

(a)

Details	Debit £	Credit £
Irrecoverable debt expense	950	
Sale ledger control account		950

(b)

£	1,000

Workings

£5,000/5 years = £1,000 per annum, full year's charge in the year of acquisition.

(c)

Details	Debit £	Credit £
Depreciation expense	1,000	
Accumulated depreciation		1,000

(d) The four enhancing qualitative characteristics are comparability, verifiability, timeliness and understandability.

(e)

Details	£	Details	£
Balance b/d	660	Drawings	750
Office Expenses	90	Balance c/d	0
Total	750	Total	750

The rent error will not be reflected in the suspense account as it is a reversal of entries error, and will still allow the trial balance to balance.

Task 2.4

(a)

Suspense account

Details	£	Details	£
Balance b/d	2,500	Drawings	2,000
Sales	500	Insurance	1,000
		Balance c/d	0
	3,000		3,000

(b)

£	1,500

Workings

(£8,000 – £500)/ 5 years

(c)

	Initial trial balance		Adjustments		Revised trial balance	
	Debit £	Credit £	Debit £	Credit £	Debit £	Credit £
Sales		195,500		500		196,000
Purchases	143,250				143,250	
Opening inventory	10,000				10,000	
Closing inventory	13,500	13,500			13,500	13,500
Office expenses	750				750	
Insurance	1,400		1,000		2,400	
Drawings	24,000		2,000		26,000	
Trade receivable	1,200				1,200	
Trade payable		1,350				1,350
Accruals		3,200				3,200

	Initial trial balance		Adjustments		Revised trial balance	
	Debit £	Credit £	Debit £	Credit £	Debit £	Credit £
Prepayments	900				900	
Capital		70,000				70,000
Cash at bank	86,050			8,000	78,050	
Suspense	2,500			2,500		
Motor vehicle			8,000		8,000	
Depreciation expense			1,500		1,500	
Accumulated depreciation				1,500		1,500
	283,550	283,550	12,500	12,500	285,550	285,550

(d)

£	126,250

Workings

Sales	196,000
Less	
Opening Inventory	10,000
Purchases	143,250
Less: Closing inventory	(13,500)
	(139,750)
Gross profit	56,250

Assessment objective 3 – Ethics for Accountants/Final Accounts Preparation

Task 3.1

(a) | £ | 31,250 |

Workings

	Carrying amount £	£
Aygosh	100,000 × 0.25 = 25,000	25,000
Scrawler B	25,000 × 0.25 = 6,250	6,250
Total depreciation expense		31,250

Note: No depreciation is charged on Masher A as it was disposed of during the year and company policy is to charge a full year in the year of acquisition and none in the year of disposal.

(b)

	Debit £	Credit £
Bank and cash	20,000	
Non-current assets – cost		85,000
Non-current asset – accumulated depreciation	70,000	
Profit and loss account		5,000

(c)

Year	Cash flow £	Discount factor 6%	Discounted cash flow £
0	(105,000)	1.000	(105,000)
1	43,400	0.943	40,926
2	52,300	0.890	46,547
3	54,800	0.840	46,032
			28,505

(d) The Gruncher 30 has a higher net present value, so would appear to be the better investment. However, it also has a significantly higher initial cost, and only has a useful life of 3 years, while the Boggler 25 has a useful life of 5 years.

Task 3.2

(a)

£	5,500

Workings

Cash at bank

Account	£	Account	£
Balance b/d	10,000	Motor expenses	650
Receipts from customers	36,000	Drawings (balancing figure)	5,500
		Payments to suppliers	25,000
		Balance c/d	14,850
Total	46,000	Total	46,000

(b) Receipts from customers £36,000

Mark up on cost is 25%, therefore $100/125 \times £36,000 = £28,800$ cost of sales in the period

(c) Closing inventory (units) = $4,000 + 6,500 - (4 \times 2,500) = 500$ units

Under the FIFO basis, closing inventory would be valued using the most recent cost of £12.50 per unit, given a closing inventory cost of £6,250.

(d)

Advantages	Disadvantages
It is a logical method to use as the oldest inventory is likely to be sold first.	The cost used to value inventory may change frequently leading to volatility.
It is an acceptable method under accounting standards, so can be used in the annual financial statements.	Each batch of inventory purchased needs to be record to ensure the correct costs are used.
Closing inventory cost will be very similar to replacement cost	

Task 3.3

(a) The accruals basis requires costs to be matched to the accounting period to which they relate, irrespective of when the payment was made. The call charges all related to calls made during the year ended 31 December 20X6.

However, the line rental charge relates to both the year ended 31 December 20X6 (December) and the year ended 31 December 20X7 (January, February 20X7).

Irrespective of when the invoice was settled (28 December 20X6), the part of the invoice that related to the year ended 31 December 20X7 should be recorded as a prepayment at 31 December 20X6. When the prepayment is reversed in the year ended 31 December 20X7, this will result in the correct expense being recorded in that financial year.

The payment date of the invoice is irrelevant under the accruals basis.

(b) The correct answer is D.

Two months or $2/3 \times £1,800 = £1,200$ has been prepaid. A prepayment is a reduction, or credit to the expense and a prepayment asset (debit) is created.

(c) Fixed costs are costs that remain the same irrespective of activity level. The line rental cost is an example of a fixed cost.

Variable costs are costs that increase as activity increases. The call charges are variable costs as they are charged at £0.06 per minute.

Assessment objective 4 – Ethics for Accountants/Final Accounts Preparation

Task 4.1

(a) Goodwill is the excess of the value of a business over its individual assets and liabilities. Goodwill may arise as a result of a number of factors, such as the reputation of the business or the skills of its management. As goodwill is intangible it can be very difficult to value and therefore is normally excluded from assets in the statement of financial position.

(b) The objectivity principle is most at risk when valuing goodwill as there can be a temptation for the valuer to be biased and place a too high figure for the goodwill figure. A possible safeguard here can be to have an independent valuer who should not be influenced when arriving at a valuation.

(c)

To: Maria Lemieux
From: An Accountant
Date: Today
Subject: Becoming a partnership

Dear Maria,

Thank you for your question regarding partnerships, I have addressed the key points below:

Advantages

- An opportunity for you to bring additional capital and expertise into the business.

- Having a partnership arrangement can also help to expand the business by taking on new clients or customers.

- You may be able to diversify into new areas of business, such as designing the sportswear rather than just acting as a retailer of existing brands.

Disadvantages

- Increased potential for disagreements between partners over business strategy and decision making.

- Any profits from the business must be shared between the partners, which initially may reduce the money you receive from your existing, established business.

- A partnership also has the same status as a sole trader with unlimited liability and this can be seen as disadvantage for the partners as they can become liable for the activities of the other partner or partners.

Potential safeguards and next steps

- Draw up a partnership agreement which sets out the terms and conditions, including any salaries, capital invested at the outset and the profit sharing proportions.

- Consider looking at becoming an LLP (Limited liability partnership) as this can offer additional safeguards like those of a limited company.

If you have any further questions, please let me know.

An Accountant

Task 4.2

(a) The ethical principle most at risk in these circumstances is professional competence and due care. The professional competence and due care principle states that members must possess the required level of knowledge and skills to complete tasks in hand.

(b) The most robust and immediate safeguard Jemima can put in place here is not to complete this task until she has developed the necessary skills and knowledge to complete it to the standard expected.

The skills and knowledge can be obtained by a combination of the following examples of continuing professional development methods:

(i)   College and online courses
(ii)   Internal training
(iii)   Professional body seminars
(iv)   Professional journals
(v)   Peer learning
(vi)   Internet research

(c) The key differences between companies and sole traders can be outlined as follows (select any FIVE from the following):

- There are specific accounting standards that apply to companies and not to sole traders.

- For companies, the formats of the statement of profit or loss and statement of financial position are standardised with required headings and terminology. Sole traders have some flexibility on layouts that can be used.

BPP
LEARNING MEDIA

- Companies are obliged to produce additional statements. An example is the cash flow statement. There is no legislative obligation for a sole trader to produce a cash flow.

- There are strict public filing rules and deadlines for companies to adhere to.

- Tax on profit is included in a company's financial statements but does not appear in a sole traders financial statements.

- Non-current assets are shown net of depreciation on the face of a company's financial statements. This is not normally the case for sole traders.

- Companies are required to prepare notes to the accounts so that accounting policies and other information can be disclosed to users. Sole traders do not have a requirement for this additional disclosure.

Task 4.3

(a) The threats most involved here are self-interest and self-review. This is because there can be a self-interest in making claims for non-existent expenses and a self-review threat as the same person is effectively reviewing their expense claim.

(b) A simple safeguard would be to reintroduce two members to staff to raise and review expense claims. There is less risk when two individuals have to be in collusion to facilitate a fraud. Another safeguard can be to rotate staff who are responsible for accounting for expense claims. This can reduce the risk of one person to have total control over a function and can help to identify any discrepancies when new staff take over responsibility.

(c) The contents of a partnership agreement can include the following:

The capital that each partner is required to initially invest into the business. This may include a minimum balance to be retained in the business.

If any interest is payable on balances on the partners' capital accounts. The agreement will also state the rate of interest and when to be received.

How profits are to be shared among partners. This profit share ratio will need to be updated when there is a change of partners or if it is agreed that the profit share should be amended.

Agreement on whether drawings can be made from the partnership. If drawings can be made then there may also be agreement on the date when drawings can be made.

Whether interest is chargeable on any drawings made by the partners. The agreement will also state the rate of interest and when to be charged.

The agreement will need to specify the salaries to be paid to partners. There can be differences in the amount of salaries paid to partners due to experience, qualifications or the amount of work put into the partnership business.

Task 4.4

(a) Materiality is a concept that provides a cut-off value on how transactions are to be treated in the financial statements. An example can be when identifying whether an expenditure should be capitalised as a non-current asset in the statement of financial position or written-off as an expense in the statement of profit or loss. A materiality policy may set the materiality level at £500 so office expenditure under this amount would be an expense and anything over this threshold treated as a non-current asset. Different businesses will have a different level of materiality. What is material for a small business may not be for a larger business. A useful rule to keep in mind is if a misstatement or omission of an item changes a user's view of results then this item is likely to be material.

(b) The colleagues' statement is incorrect as materiality levels do not apply to criminal acts of money laundering. The Latin term for this is that there is no de minimis rule to exempt from the law. In this instance this matter should be reported to the business's Nominated Officer. The colleague appears to have an interest in not pursuing this issue further so may be involved in the fraud in some way. In which case care needs to be taken not to tip-off that this is being reported.

(c) The ethical principle most at risk here is confidentiality as any information must not be disclosed without proper authority. Not only does Amy have a professional responsibility to keep information confidential but also there is a legal requirement under the data protection regulations to keep individual information secure.

The threat most evident is intimidation as the customer is threatening to withdraw his custom if Amy does not comply with his request.

(d) Amy must refuse this request and to maintain complete confidentiality regarding customer details.

If Amy was to contact each customer and ask for specific authorisation to release information about them in this way then it can be acceptable. Other times when information can be disclosed is when it is in the public interest and if there is a legal requirement to do so.

Task 4.5

(a) A conflict of interest is where an individual's objectivity may become threatened due to the circumstances of an assignment or relationship. An example can be where an accountant is acting on behalf of two clients whose business interests overlap.

(b) The accountant will need to identify if any conflict of interest threats exist. If threats do exist and are considered to be significant then safeguards need to be put in place to reduce those threats to an acceptable level.

(c) There is a clear conflict of interest here as Jaz is preparing the accounts for both parties and is aware of sensitive information that is relevant to the loan A has made to B. In these circumstances Jaz must remain independent and complete any work with objectivity and without bias. A principle at threat here is confidentiality and Jaz needs to be very careful in not disclosing confidential information to either party.

The safeguards that Jaz can put in place may include:

- Inform both clients that she is acting for both clients.

- Obtain written consent to act on behalf of both clients. This may include confidentiality agreements.

- Investigate whether a colleague may be able to handle the work of one of the clients.

- Have a senior partner independently review Jaz's work to ensure independence and confidentiality is being observed.

- Ensure that any information is kept confidential within Jaz's office by having a 'Chinese Wall' to keep information secure or a code of conduct on access.

- In the last resort if all other safeguards are still not adequate resign from one of the assignments.

Task 4.6

(a) A limited company is financed by equity and this can be made up of share capital where shares have been issued and also accumulated profits that have been added to the reserves of the company.

Normally the owners of the business, the shareholders, will extract money from the company in the form of dividends paid from accumulated profits made by the company.

This is different to a sole trader or partnership arrangement where the owner or owners invest capital into the business and subsequently withdraw capital in the form of drawings.

(b) The two ethical principles most affected here are professional competence and due care and professional behaviour. The accountant did not take due care when not checking the equity figure was correct. Professional behaviour is also threatened as reports in the financial press and other media will bring disrepute to the accountancy profession.

Observing that equity had increased by 80 times from the previous year the accountant may have had some doubts over the accuracy of this increase.

(c) Professional scepticism is where a professional person may question the accuracy or validity of any information or evidence that is made available to them in the completion of their work. As the equity figure is a material amount in the financial statements the accountant should have initially questioned whether the £2m figure was correct and should have planned their work to obtain evidence to substantiate this figure.

Task 4.7

(a) The two relevant accounting standards here are:

IAS 2 *Inventories*

IAS 16 *Property, plant and equipment*

(b) The ethical principle most at risk when being out of date in knowledge and skills is professional competence and due care.

(c) An accountant can keep their skills and knowledge up to date by completing regular continuing professional development (CPD). Evidence of complying with the professional competence and due care can be achieved by keeping a CPD Log to record and explain any CPD activities completed. It is important to note that professional bodies do require completing of CPD and if a member is found to be in non-compliance then it is likely the body will take disciplinary action against the member.

If it is found that a member's work has been completed without all the necessary skills required this may also result in breach of contract with the risk of being sued for negligence by an injured party who may have suffered a loss due to sub-standard work.

Assessment objective 5 – Management Accounting: Costing

Task 5.1

(a)

Year	Year 0 £	Year 1 £	Year 2 £	Year 3 £	Year 4 £
Capital expenditure	(240,000)				
Sales revenue		200,000	220,000	231,000	237,930
Variable costs		100,000	110,000	115,500	118,965
Fixed costs		20,000	20,000	20,000	20,000
Net cash flows		80,000	90,000	95,500	98,965
PV factors	1.000	0.917	0.842	0.772	0.708
Discounted cash flows (to nearest £)	(240,000)	73,360	75,780	73,726	70,067
Net present value					52,933

(b) The payback period is 2 years and 9 months.

Year	Cumulative cashflow £
1	80,000
2	170,000
3	265,500
4	364,465

Payback period is 2 years and (£70,000/£95,500 × 12 months) and 8.8 months, rounded to 9 months.

Task 5.2

	Original budget £ 40,000 units	Flexed budget £ 45,000 units	Actual results £ 45,000 units	Variances £
Sales revenue	920,000	1,035,000	1,040,000	(5,000)
Direct materials	520,000	585,000	562,500	22,500
Direct labour	45,000	50,625	54,600	(3,975)
Variable overheads	55,000	61,875	71,300	(9,425)
Fixed overheads	26,000	26,000	30,300	(4,300)
Operating profit	300,000		351,600	

Task 5.3

Budgeted overheads	Basis of apportionment	Production A	Production B	Administration	Total
Depreciation	PPE carrying amount	101,867	68,675	19,458	190,000
Rent and rates	Floor space	170,414	189,586		360,000
Power	Floor space	115,030	127,970		243,000
Production supervisors	No. of supervisors	81,667	58,333		140,000
General administration				463,000	463,000
Subtotal		**468,978**	**444,564**	**482,458**	**1,396,000**
Reapportion administration (55%/45%)		265,352	217,106	(482,458)	
Total		734,330	661,670		1,396,000

Assessment objective 6 – Advanced Bookkeeping/Final Accounts Preparation

Task 6.1

Mr I Jones

Statement of profit or loss for the year ended 31 May 20X6

	£	£
Sales revenue		280,480
Opening inventory	7,800	
Purchases	150,800	
Less: closing inventory	(9,000)	
Cost of sales		(149,600)
Gross profit		130,880
Less expenses:		
General expenses	63,800	
Administration costs	3,900	
IT equipment depreciation	850	
Wages	42,000	
		(110,550)
Net profit		20,330

Task 6.2

	Karen £	Jake £	Saffron £	Total £
Salaries	11,400	14,400	9,600	35,400
Interest on capital	1,000	1,200	600	2,800
	12,400	15,600	10,200	38,200
Profit available for distribution (20% / 65% / 15%)	28,360	92,170	21,270	141,800
	40,760	107,770	31,470	180,000

Task 6.3

(a) Current accounts

Account	Andrew £	Brown £	Carter £	Account	Andrew £	Brown £	Carter £
Drawings W1	30,000	38,000	45,000	Balance b/d	1,160	420	5,570
Balance c/d	25,892	10,054	14,204	Salaries	15,000	18,000	24,000
				Interest on capital	2,860	1,980	1,980
				Share of profit or loss	36,872	27,654	27,654
Total	55,892	48,054	59,204		55,892	48,054	59,204

Working

Drawings:

Andrew: £2,500 × 12 months = £30,000

Drawings for Brown and Carter taken from question.

(b) Who would usually be the most appropriate first person to raise this with?

your immediate supervisor   or   employee helpline .

(c) **Are these statements relating to whistleblowing true or false?**

Statement	True	False
Employees are protected under the Public Information Disclosure Act provided that they have acted in good faith and the belief is that the environment is being damaged	✓	
You should start the whistleblowing process as soon as illegal activity is suspected.		✓
The fundamental principle of confidentiality is not breached, if the disclosure is in the public interest.	✓	
If the organisation has an ethics committee, this should be approached before getting to the whistleblowing stage.	✓	

Task 6.4

(a)

	Cost £	Accumulated depreciation £	Carrying amount £
Non-current assets			
Fixtures & Fittings	24,500	8,550	15,950
Motor vehicles	48,000	29,800	18,200
Current assets			
Inventory	43,500		
Trade receivables *(W1)*	32,250		
Prepayments	1,250		
Cash and cash equivalents	11,950		
		88,950	

	Cost £	Accumulated depreciation £	Carrying amount £
Current liabilities			
Trade payables	40,800		
VAT	3,050		
Accruals	1,000		
		44,850	
Net current assets			44,100
Net assets			**78,250**
Financed by:			
Capital			74,300
Profit for the year			22,950
Less:			
Drawings			(19,000)
			78,250

Workings

W1: 35,450 – 3,200 = 32,250

(b) **The two fundamental qualitative characteristics of financial information, according to the IASB's *Conceptual Framework* are:**

| relevance | and | faithful representation |

(c)

	✓
The effect of transactions being recognised when they occur	
That the business will continue in operation for the foreseeable future	✓
To ensure similar businesses can be compared to allow for investors to assess them	
To ensure the financial statements have been prepared on time	

Task 6.5

	£	£
Sales revenue		171,800
Less:		
Opening inventory	20,100	
Purchases	122,500	
Less: Closing inventory	(21,750)	
Cost of goods sold		(120,850)
Gross profit		50,950
Less:		
Depreciation expense	5,125	
Irrecoverable debt expense (from additional information)	475	
Electricity	1,025	
Insurance	900	
Motor expenses	1,550	
Miscellaneous expense	750	
Rent	1,700	
Telephone	975	
Repairs and maintenance	1,250	
Total expenses		13,750
Profit/loss for the year		37,200

AAT AQ2016 ASSESSMENTS
LEVEL 3 SYNOPTIC ASSESSMENT

You are advised to attempt the AAT Practice Assessments online from the AAT website. This will ensure you are prepared for how the assessment will be presented on the AAT's system when you attempt the real assessment. The assessments are called:

Advanced diploma synoptic assessment (ADSY) – practice assessment 1 and **Advanced diploma synoptic assessment (ADSY) – practice assessment 2**, with the assessments using the AAT software. Please note that these are not marked, however, AAT provide pdf versions of the answers for you to review your responses.

Please access the assessment using the address below:

https://www.aat.org.uk/learning-portal

The AAT may call the assessments on their website, under Study support resources, either a 'practice assessment' or 'sample assessment'.

BPP PRACTICE ASSESSMENT 1
LEVEL 3 SYNOPTIC ASSESSMENT

Time allowed: 2 hours and 30 minutes

PRACTICE ASSESSMENT 1

Advanced Diploma Synoptic Assessment (ADSY) BPP practice assessment 1

Task 1 is based on a workplace scenario separate to the rest of the assessment.

Task 2 to **Task 6** is based on the scenario of Clodlands partnership which is as follows:

> You are Paula, a part-qualified accounting technician employed by Radcliffe & Rutherfords, an accountancy firm.
>
> Friends Chipo and Charlie have recently begun to trade through a new partnership, Clodlands which owns and lets several areas of land including two houses.

Task 1 (15 marks)

The following statements have been made by trainee accountants in relation to the AAT *Code of Professional Ethics* and the fundamental principles.

(a)   Show whether the below statements are true or false.

Statement	True	False
'It doesn't matter whether or not people might think my actions are unethical, it is whether or not I actually am that counts'.		
'As long as I comply with the principle of integrity, compliance with the other principles will be implied as a result'.		
'The ethical code applies to my role as a professional and my working life. My private life, on the other hand, is just that – private!'		
'As a professional accountant, it is more important for me to be ethical as I work in the public interest.'		

(4 marks)

Professional accountants are required to undertake continuing professional development (CPD).

(b) **Show whether or not the *Code of Professional Ethics* specifically requires an AAT member to take each of the following actions in order to act in line with the principle of objectivity.**

Statement	True	False
As an accountant in practice, if a member undertakes services for two clients working in the same industry, the member must always resign from one of the engagements.		
If a member has a family relative working in a managerial position at a company they provide services for, the member should alert their line manager.		
Your close friend, Jill, has become a director at one of the clients you work for. It is recommended that an alternative manager at your firm works with Jill's business instead.		

(3 marks)

Marion, a professional accountant in practice, gives Larch Ltd an opinion on the application of accounting principles to the company's specific transactions. Marion knew that she was forming her opinion on the basis of inadequate information.

(c) **Which ONE of the following fundamental principles have been breached by Marion?**

Action	✓
Confidentiality	
Professional competence and due care	
Fairness	

(2 marks)

Dipika is an accountant employed by Natural Beauty, a company which develops, manufactures and sells luxury bath and body products. One of the company's top selling products is a body polish which it claims uses all natural ingredients. The exfoliating quality of the polish is achieved using sea salt and fine sand.

During the course of her work, Dipika discovers that, in order to reduce costs, the company has begun to replace some of the sand with microbeads. Microbeads are tiny plastic beads which pollute both the ocean and the food chain for human consumption. The use of microbeads is banned in a number of countries, but they have not yet been banned by the country in which Natural Beauty operates. They are not 'natural' ingredients and the packaging has not been updated to reflect this.

(d) **Show whether the below statements are true or false.**

Statement	True	False
Natural Beauty may have broken the law.		
Natural Beauty has acted unethically.		

(2 marks)

(e) **Which ONE of the below actions should Dipika now take?**

Action	✓
Take the issue directly to the press as it is in the public interest to disclose this via the media	
She should do nothing, the issue is not of a financial nature and therefore outside the scope of her expertise and ethical requirements	
Discuss the findings with her immediate manager and share her concerns regarding the company's use of microbeads	

(2 marks)

(f) **If Dipika discloses this issue through appropriate channels, either internally or externally, would any protection against dismissal be offered to Dipika under the Public Information Disclosure Act 1998 (PIDA)?**

Action	✓
No, as disclosure of the matter would be inappropriate in this situation.	
Yes, as she has reasonable grounds to believe that the environment is being damaged and disclosure was made in good faith.	
No, PIDA only protects individuals who are disclosing serious organised crimes such as money laundering.	

(2 marks)

Task 2 (12 marks)

This task is based on the workplace scenario of the Clodlands partnership.

On reviewing Clodland's sales day books, you have found three errors:

Sales ledger control account

		£			£
01/06	Balance b/d	32,300	30/6	Bank and cash	23,500
30/06	Sales	17,800			
			30/6	Balance c/d	26,600
		50,100			50,100

- A sales invoice of £2,700 had not been posted on 29 June.

- A customer who owed £3,600 had been declared bankrupt on 25 June, and it is unlikely that the debt will be recovered.

- An error was made by the credit control clerk, which meant that a cash receipt for an invoice was incorrectly recorded as £1,730, when the invoice was actually for £1,370.

You prepare journals to correct these errors.

(a) **What is the journal to correct the error made by the credit controller?**

		£
Debit	▼	360
Credit	▼	360

Picklist:

Sales ledger control account
Bank and cash
Sales day book
Sales returns book

(2 marks)

(b) **Which of the following correctly describes the type of error made by the credit control clerk?**

	✓
Error of omission	
Error of original entry	
Error of principle	

(1 mark)

(c) **In order to account for the irrecoverable debt, which side of the sales ledger control account will the entry be accounted for?**

	✓
Debit	
Credit	

(1 mark)

(d) **What is the revised carried down balance after the correction of the errors on the sales ledger control account as at 30 June?**

£

(2 marks)

(e) **Which ONE of the following statements about a Limited Liability Partnership is NOT correct?**

Description	✓
An LLP is a separate legal entity.	
The LLP must be registered with the Registrar of Companies.	
There is no upper limit to the number of partners a LLP can have.	
The LLP must file annual returns, accounts and an annual corporation tax return.	

(2 marks)

You have discovered that Charlie has been charging VAT on invoices, even though Clodlands is not yet registered for VAT. When questioned, he declared that he 'didn't see the problem as Clodlands paid VAT on supplier invoices anyway'. You have informed Chipo, but she does not mind either.

(f) **Complete the following statement by selecting ONE of the options below.**

The accountant should disclose this information NEXT to which of the following parties?

	✓
The Nominated Officer at Radcliffe's and Rutherfords	
HMRC	
National Crime Agency	

(1 marks)

You discover that Charlie has begun training for his AAT qualification and has signed up as a student with the AAT.

(g) **Which ONE of the following statements is correct about AAT disciplinary procedures?**

	✓
Charlie will not be exposed to disciplinary proceedings because he has not taken all of his exams yet.	
The Code of Professional Ethics is only enforceable for fully qualified members of the AAT.	
Charlie may disciplined if he fails to comply with AAT CPD requirements.	

(1 marks)

(h) **Complete the following sentence by selecting the correct word from the picklist.**

The AAT has a Continuing Professional Development (CPD) cycle which comprises four steps.

These are assess, plan, [_____▼] and evaluate.

Picklist:

action
consider
engage
mitigate

(2 marks)

· ·

Task 3 (13 marks)

This task is based on the workplace scenario of the Clodlands partnership.

The partnership started trading on 1 July 20X7. Extracts from the draft trial balance at 30 June 20X7 are as follows:

Account	Debit £	Credit £
Cost of sales	96,000	
Land and buildings – cost	2,450,000	
Office equipment – cost	8,100	
Administrative expenses	24,600	
Finance costs	30,000	
Revenue		193,000
Bank loan		500,000

On 1 July 20X6, Clodlands purchased land, including two houses. The land had a cost of £1,600,000 and the houses cost £850,000 in total.

The depeciation policy of Clodlands is as follows:

- land is not depreciated
- buildings are depreciated on a straight-line basis over an expected useful life of 30 years
- office equipment is depreciated on a diminishing balance basis at 25%

Assets are depreciated on a monthly basis, with a full month's charge in the month of acquisition and no charge in the month of disposal. Land and buildings depreciation charges should be recorded in cost of sales. Office equipment depreciation is recorded as administrative expenses.

(a) Explain the purpose of depreciation for tangible non-current assets.

(2 marks)

(b)   Calculate the depreciation expenses for Clodlands for the year ended 30 June 20X7. You must show all workings.

(4 marks)

Clodlands received a loan from the bank. One of the conditions of the loan was that the bank needs to see quarterly management accounts and the annual financial statements.

(c)   Explain why the bank might want to see these documents.

(2 marks)

(d) Calculate the gross profit and operating profit for Clodlands for the year ended 30 June 20X7 after adjusting for depreciation. You must show all workings. Operating profit is profit before finance charges (and tax).

(4 marks)

(e) The depreciation charge on Clodland's buildings is an example of a:

	✓
Fixed overhead	
Variable overhead	

(1 mark)

....

Task 4 (15 marks)

This task is based on the workplace scenario of the Clodlands partnership. You are Paula, a part-qualified accounting technician employed by Radcliffe & Rutherfords, an accountancy firm.

It is Monday morning when the partner, Mr Rutherford, calls you into his office for a private meeting. He explains that he has a number of expenses relating to personal expenditure that he would like to put through the company's books of accounts. He hands you a file containing a year's worth of private bank statements and requests you to identify any expenditure relating to his expensive family holidays and post as an expense to the business travel account.

Your response is you have learnt at college that only valid business expenditure should be recorded through the business's books of account. However, his reasoning is that the holidays are there to help him relax from the stress of running a business so it is only fair this is recorded as a business expense.

The director implies that as a thank you he may able to obtain two tickets for two seats for the finals at a tennis tournament. When you return to your desk you complete an Internet search and are surprised to discover these tickets are currently selling in excess of £500 each.

(a) **Outline any potential ethical issues that this work request can bring. In your answer refer to the *Code of Professional Ethics* highlighting specific threats that may apply.**

(6 marks)

(b) **State your decision regarding the request from the partner and state any further action you would be required to take.**

(2 marks)

You have received the following email from one of your colleagues:

To: You@.accounts

From: Colleague@.accounts

Hi,

I am a new joiner at the partnership and will be working on the partnership end of year financial statements. I have just started my accountancy studies and have only covered sole traders. We have not covered the types of accounts and financial statements used in partnerships. This is all new to me!

Please can you help me get started?

Kind regards,

Colleague

(c) Reply to your colleague outlining the accounts and statements used in a partnership arrangement. Your answer should be suitable for someone with no knowledge of partnerships.

(7 marks)

Task 5 (12 marks)

This task is based on the workplace scenario of the Clodlands partnership.

A draft budget for the year ended 30 June 20X8 has been produced.

	£	£
Revenue:		
Land rental income	145,000	
House rental income	60,000	
		205,000
Fixed costs:		
Staff costs	80,000	
Repairs	15,000	
Depreciation	30,000	
Administration overheads	30,000	
		(155,000)
Operating profit		50,000

Chipo has asked for your help to revise the budget. Charlie and her have decided that they are going to apply a 2% increase to rental income for both land and the houses.

They are considering the acquisition of a two new properties. Relevant details are as follows:

	New House A	New House B
Proposed acquisition date	1 October 20X7	1 January 20X8
Purchase cost	£400,000	£600,000
	£ per annum	£ per annum
Expected rental income	35,000	50,000
Additional costs		
Staff costs	15,000	25,000
Administration overheads	2,000	9,000
Repairs	5,000	12,000

The new properties would be depreciated on a straight-line basis over 30 years, with a full month of deprecation charged in the month of acquisition.

(a) **Complete the following table to include the suggested changes above and revise the proposed budget. Show your answers to the nearest whole pound.**

(12 marks)

	Draft budget £	Rental increase £	New House A £	New House B £	Revised budget £
Revenue:					
Land rental income	145,000	147,900			
House rental income	60,000	61,200		25,000	
	205,000				
Fixed costs:					
Staff costs	80,000		11,250		
Repairs	15,000				
Depreciation	30,000				
Administration overheads	30,000			4,500	
	155,000				
Operating profit	50,000				

Task 6 (13 marks)

This task is based on the workplace scenario of the Clodlands partnership.

- The depreciation charge for the year for office equipment of £2,025 was correctly posted to the accumulated depreciation account, however, no expense has been posted in the statement of profit or loss.

- Clodlands received £300 in respect of an invoice from Most Lotus on 30 June 20X7. This has not been reflected in the receivables ledger control accounts or the bank.

- A purchase invoice in respect of electricity charges was incorrectly posted to the electricity expense account as £850. The correct amount of £580 was posted to the purchase ledger.

Requirements:

(a) Complete the extract from the extended trial balance, making any adjustments necessary for the items above.

(9 marks)

	Trial balance		Adjustments		SOPL		SOFP	
	Dr £	Cr £	Dr £	Cr £	Dr £	Cr £	Dr £	Cr £
Bank	6,930							
Suspense	1,755							
Trade payables		3,000						
Trade receivables	3,080							
Electricity	1,620							
Depreciation – office equipment								

Clodlands made a profit for the year of £8,540. Chipo and Charlie have taken salaries of £2,000 and £2,500 respectively. They both receive interest of 4% on the capital the introduced to the business, which was £60,000 each. Chipo and Charlie share profits or losses equally.

(b)   Complete the partnership appropriation table.

	Chipo £	Charlie £	Total £
Salaries			
Interest on capital			
Residue			

(4 marks)

BPP PRACTICE ASSESSMENT 1
LEVEL 3 SYNOPTIC ASSESSMENT

ANSWERS

Advanced Diploma Synoptic Assessment (ADSY) BPP practice assessment 1

Task 1 (15 marks)

(a)

Statement	True	False
'It doesn't matter whether or not people might think my actions are unethical, it is whether or not I actually am that counts.'		✓
'As long as I comply with the principle of integrity, compliance with the other principles will be implied as a result.'		✓
'The ethical code applies to my role as a professional and my working life. My private life, on the other hand, is just that – private!'		✓
'As a professional accountant, it is more important for me to be ethical as I work in the public interest.'	✓	

(b)

	True	False
As an accountant in practice, if a member undertakes services for two clients working in the same industry, the member must always resign from one of the engagements.		✓
If a member has a family relative working in a managerial position at a company they provide services for, the member should alert their line manager.	✓	
Your close friend, Jill, has become a director at one of the clients you work for. It is recommended that an alternative manager at your firm works with Jill's business instead.		✓

Resignation would only be required if no other safeguard was available to the member. Alternative safeguards would be required and the clients made aware.

There is a familiarity threat to the member's objectivity and this should be raised with the manager internally in the first instance.

Even though work discussions may not take place, a member should be seen to be maintaining the principle of objectivity, so safeguards should be put in place to show that no breach can occur.

(c)

Action	✓
Confidentiality	
Professional competence and due care	✓
Fairness	

Confidentiality and fairness are Nolan Principles

(d)

Statement	True	False
Natural Beauty may have broken the law.		✓
Natural Beauty has acted unethically.	✓	

The replacement of one of the ingredients is not against the law in the country that Natural Beauty operates, however, by misleading their customers and not informing them of the substitution this can be deemed to be unethical behaviour. As Natural Beauty claims to use all natural ingredients this is not the behaviour that their customers would expect from the business.

(e)

Action	✓
Take the issue directly to the press as it is in the public interest to disclose this via the media.	
She should do nothing, the issue is not of a financial nature and therefore outside the scope of her expertise and ethical requirements.	
Discuss the findings with her immediate manager and share her concerns regarding the company's use of microbeads.	✓

Dipka should discuss her concerns with her immediate supervisor in the first instance before any further action is taken.

(f)

Action	✓
No, as disclosure of the matter would be inappropriate in this situation.	
Yes, as she has reasonable grounds to believe that the environment is being damaged and disclosure was made in good faith.	✓
No, PIDA only protects individuals who are disclosing serious organised crimes such as money laundering.	

Task 2 (15 marks)

(a)

		£
Debit	Sales ledger control account	360
Credit	Bank and cash	360

(b)

Description	✓
Error of omission	
Error of original entry	✓
Error of principle	

(c)

	✓
Debit	
Credit	✓

(d)

£	26,060

Workings

		£				£
01/06	Balance b/d	32,300	30/6		Bank and cash	23,500
30/06	Sales	17,800	30/6		Irrecoverable debt	3,600
	Sales invoice (missing)	2,700				
	Error by credit control	360			Balance c/d (balancing figure)	26,060
		53,160				53,160

(e)

Description	✓
An LLP is a separate legal entity.	
The LLP must be registered with the Registrar of Companies.	
There is no upper limit to the number of partners a LLP can have.	
The LLP must file annual returns, accounts and an annual corporation tax return.	✓

Although an LLP should file annual accounts, they are not required to file a corporation tax return as this is only for companies, not partnerships.

(f)

	✓
The Nominated Officer at Radcliffe's and Rutherfords	✓
HMRC	
National Crime Agency	

The next appropriate course of action would be to raise the matter with the designated nominated officer at the firm of accountants where you work, Only then will the matter be considered before whether it should be raised with HMRC or the NCA.

(g)

	✓
Charlie will not be exposed to disciplinary proceedings because he has not taken all of his exams yet.	
The Code of Professional Ethics is only enforceable for fully qualified members of the AAT.	
Charlie may disciplined if he fails to comply with AAT CPD requirements.	✓

AAT students must also comply with the *AAT Code of Professional Ethics*. Once they are registered with the AAT, they are bound by the requirements.

(h) The AAT has a Continuing Professional Development (CPD) cycle which comprises four steps.

These are assess, plan, action and evaluate.

....

Task 3 (13 marks)

(a) Depreciation is a way of spreading the cost of a tangible non-current asset over it's useful life. It utilises the accruals principle, that the expense should be matched against the period of use.

(b)

	Cost £		Depreciation charge £
Land	1,600,000	none	0
Buildings	850,000	= 850k / 30 years	28,333
Office equipment	8,100	=25% × 8.1k	2,025

BPP
LEARNING MEDIA

(c) The bank has lent a considerable amount of money to Clodlands. They might wish to see regular management accounts and the annual financial statements to ensure that their bank loan is secure and that Clodlands will continue to be able to meet their interest and capital repayments.

(d)

	£	
Revenue	193,000	
Cost of sales	(124,333)	96,000 + 28,333 depreciation
Gross profit	68,667	
Administrative expenses	(26,625)	24,600 + 2,025 depreciation
Operating profit	42,042	

(e)

	✓
Fixed overhead	✓
Variable overhead	

....

Task 4 (15 marks)

(a) When preparing financial statements only valid business expenditure is allowed to be recorded as a business expense. This is because the business is a single entity (not legal entity) and its financial affairs need to be kept separate from the owner or owners own personal dealings. Recording invalid expenses would misrepresent the results of the company and would also understate taxable profits. This can be viewed as money laundering and is a criminal offence. If the partners' own family holiday costs were recorded through the partnership this would be dishonest and a breach of the integrity principle. There is a self-interest threat to the objectivity principle as I may be influenced by the promise of the tennis tickets. Due to the value of the tennis tickets this could be seen as a bribe and is a criminal offence under the Bribery Act.

(b) I must refuse to comply with the partner's request and as this can be seen as money laundering, I need to prepare an internal report to disclose this matter to the partnership Nominated officer.

A reasonable third party would view the tennis tickets as a bribe and must not be accepted.

(c) To: Colleague@accounts

From: You@accounts

Subject: Partnership accounts

Hi,

Welcome to the partnership and thank you for contacting on this matter.

A partnership has many similarities to a sole trader as accounting principles and concepts will be the same however there are some important differences to account for two or more people sharing the business.

Here is a summary of the important differences.

Capital accounts

When an individual starts a business they will have a capital account to record the money invested in the business. This is similar to partnerships where each partner will have a separate capital account to record permanent capital invested in the partnership. An important point here is that partnership capital accounts only record long term capital investment.

Current accounts

Each partner will also have separate current account and these are used to record shorter term transactions arising from the partnership and show amounts owing to or from the partnership. Typical credit entries on a current account can be salaries, interest on capital and share in any profits made. These are amounts owed to the individual partner. A typical debit entry will be drawings where a partner extracts money from the partnership similar to a sole trader taking drawings from a business. Any drawings made by a partner will reduce the amount owed to the partner by the partnership.

Appropriation account

The appropriation account shows the total amount of profit made by the partnership with deductions for partner's salaries and interest on capital and adjustments for any interest charged on drawings. The residual amount is then available for sharing between the partners in the agreed partnership sharing ratios.

Statement of financial position

This financial statement shows the assets and liabilities of the partnership. The bottom part of the statement of financial position will show the current and capital accounts for each partner.

I hope this helps.

Please let me know if I can clarify any of the above.

Regards,

Task 5 (12 marks)

	Draft budget £	Rental increase £	New House A £	New House B £	Revised budget £
Revenue:					
Land rental income	145,000	147,900			147,900
House rental income	60,000	61,200	26,250	25,000	112,450
	205,000				260,350
Fixed costs:					
Staff costs	80,000		11,250	12,500	103,750
Repairs	15,000		3,750	6,000	24,750
Depreciation	30,000		10,000	10,000	50,000
Administration overheads	30,000		1,500	4,500	36,000
	155,000				214,500
Operating profit	50,000				45,850

New House A & B – Rental, staff costs, repairs and admin costs are 75%/50% of the figures given to reflect 9 months / 6 months of income and expenses.

Task 6 (13 marks)

(a)

	Trial balance		Adjustments		SOPL		SOFP	
	Dr £	Cr £	Dr £	Cr £	Dr £	Cr £	Dr £	Cr £
Bank	6,930		300				7,230	
Suspense	1,755		270	2,025				
Trade payables		3,000						3,000
Trade receivables	3,080			300			2,780	
Electricity	1,620			270	1,350			
Depreciation – office equipment			2,025		2,025			

(b)

	Chipo £	Charlie £	Total £
Salaries	2,000	2,500	4,500
Interest on capital	2,400	2,400	4,800
	4,400	4,900	9,300
Residue (£8,540 - £9,300)			(760)
(50% / 50%)	(380)	(380)	
	4,020	4,520	8,540

141

BPP PRACTICE ASSESSMENT 2
LEVEL 3 SYNOPTIC ASSESSMENT

Time allowed: 2 hours and 30 minutes

Advanced Diploma Synoptic Assessment (ADSY) BPP practice assessment 2

Task 1 is based on a workplace scenario separate to the rest of the assessment.

Task 2 to **Task 6** is based on the scenario of Sauter which is as follows:

> You are Jamie, a part-qualified accounting technician employed by Broadchurch & Co, an accountancy firm.
>
> The client you are working on is Sauter, and your firm provides bookkeeping and accounting services for this business. Sauter manufactures kitchenware and is owned and managed by Micha.

Task 1 (15 marks)

(a) Complete the following sentence.

A professional accountant who complies with the law, brings no disrepute on the profession and is perceived as being ethical by other people has complied with the fundamental principle of [▼] .

Picklist:

confidentiality
integrity
objectivity
professional behaviour
professional competence and due care

(2 marks)

The requirement for ethical business practices means that sustainable development and corporate social responsibility are becoming increasingly important.

(b) Which ONE of the following is true in respect of the accountant's role in sustainable development and corporate social responsibility reporting?

Statement	✓
Sustainability and CSR are not financial matters and sit outside the remit of the professional accountant.	
Sustainability and CSR form part of the accountant's obligation to work in the public interest.	
Sustainability and CSR are only key considerations for accountants working in particular industries, such as the renewable energy industry.	

(2 marks)

Danny is a professional accountant working in practice. Whilst carrying out some work for his client, Inge, he has acted outside the limits of his professional expertise.

As a result of the work carried out by Danny, Inge has now incurred a regulatory fine.

(c)   Which ONE of the actions below would provide grounds for Inge to seek compensation from Danny?

Action	✓
Professional negligence	
Self interest	
Fraud under false representation	

(2 marks)

Sparkys Limited, a small home electricals company who you have worked with for a number of years, has unexpectedly requested your practice to help in selling a number of residential properties that they have recently acquired.

(d)   State whether customer due diligence should be carried before accepting this work.

Statement	True	False
Due diligence procedures are not necessary as this situation relates to an existing client.		
You should report this matter urgently to the relevant authorities. There is clearly something amiss.		

(2 marks)

You are a newly qualified accounting technician working in practice. Your colleague Piers has been off work sick for the past week and your line manager asks you to go through his in-tray and deal with anything that needs urgent attention.

In Piers' in-tray you find a letter addressed to Piers from one of his clients, Martin. In this letter Martin asks Piers to include a revenue figure in his tax return which is much lower than the actual revenue received by the client. Martin offers Piers 'the £1,000 you need to clear your gambling debt' in return for inclusion of this incorrect figure. Martin also suggests that if this is not done by the end of the month, he will inform the firm of the other ways in which Piers has helped him to present suitable figures in the past.

(e) Complete the following sentence.

As a result of this letter, Piers faces threats of [▼] and [▼] to his professional ethics.

Picklist:

advocacy
familiarity
intimidation
self-interest
self-review

(2 marks)

(f) State which THREE of the following of Piers' fundamental principles are threatened by this letter.

Action	✓
Integrity	
Objectivity	
Confidentiality	
Professional competence and due care	
Professional behaviour	

(3 marks)

(g) Which of the following actions would it be most appropriate for you to take on discovery of this letter?

	✓
Hide the letter back in the in-tray and pretend you never saw it; it would not do for you to get caught up in this mess	
Report the misconduct immediately to the AAT	
Discuss the situation with your immediate line manager	

(2 marks)

Task 2 (12 marks)

You are Jamie, a part-qualified accounting technician employed by Broadchurch & Co, an accountancy firm. The partner of Broadchurch & Co, Mr Tennant, has asked you to answer some queries which have come into the office from Jonas, the accounts assistant at your client, Sauter Ltd.

Sauter has purchased a new delivery van from Vans & Co using a bank loan to fund the purchase. Jonas is unsure how to account for it and explains that he has 'heard of depreciation' but doesn't understand what it is and how to calculate it.

Cost of van   £13,500
Expected scrap value   £1,500

Jonas expects to use the van for 3 years before Sauter upgrades to a bigger van.

(a) **Show the double entry for the van which Sauter has purchased in the journal below, using the picklist to select the relevant accounts.**

Account name		Amount £	Debit ✓	Credit ✓
	▼			
	▼			

Picklist:

Bank loan
Cash
Inventory
Non-current assets: vehicles
Trade payable (Vans & Co)

(2 marks)

(b) **What is the annual depreciation charge on the new van on a straight line basis?**

£	

(1 mark)

(c) **Which TWO of the following statements about depreciation are TRUE?**

	✓
Depreciation spreads the cost of an asset over its residual life	
All tangible non-current assets must be depreciated	
Depreciation is debited to retained earnings	
Accumulated depreciation reduces the carrying amount of the tangible non-current asset	

(2 marks)

Jonas is also unsure how to deal with trade receivables at the year end. The draft sales ledger control account balance at 31 December 20X8 is £62,700. There is also an allowance for doubtful debts of £1,600, however this is the figure from 31 December 20X7.

The managing director, Micha, has informed Jonas that one of Sauter's clients, LivStar, is no longer trading. Sauter has an outstanding balance in the sales ledger relating to LivStar of £6,700.

Jonas is aware that Sauter usually makes an allowance for doubtful debts based on 2% of the outstanding sales ledger control account balance.

(d) **The adjustment to deal with the irrecoverable debt from LivStar is:**

Account name		Amount £	Debit ✓	Credit ✓
	▼			
	▼			

Picklist:

Sales
Sales ledger control account
Allowance for doubtful debts
Irrecoverable debt expense
Cash

(2 marks)

(e) Which of the following statements about the allowance for doubtful debts is correct?

	✓
The allowance for doubtful debts is an expense in the statement of profit or loss	
The allowance for doubtful debts increases the trade receivables balance	
The allowance for doubtful debts reflects the possible non-payment of some receivable balances	

(1 mark)

You have calculated the allowance for doubtful debts at 31 December 20X8 to be £1,120.

(f) Complete the sentence below to show the correct treatment of the allowance for doubtful debts at 31 December 20X8.

The allowance for doubtful debts will be [　　　　　　▼] by [　　　　　　▼]

Picklist 1:

increased
decreased

Picklist 2:

£1,120
£1,600
£480

(2 marks)

Sauter are considering acquiring some new machinery through a lease agreement. You are unsure how to deal with this type of accounting.

(g) What is your next course of action?

	✓
Leave the work on this lease agreement for another colleague to find, after all, Sauter will chase if they haven't heard anything for a while	
Show a willing attitude and give it your best shot	
Consult with your line manager about the task	

(1 mark)

(h) **State the fundamental principle which is at risk in this scenario.**

	✓
Confidentiality	
Professional competence and due care	
Objectivity	

(1 mark)

Task 3 (13 marks)

Micha has recently been to a meeting of local business leaders and heard about the concept of marginal costing. She would like to know the effect of costing Sauter's products under marginal costing principles instead of full absorption costing.

You have obtained the following information about Sauter's main product:

Selling price per unit	£19
Direct materials per unit	£4
Direct labour per unit	£3
Variable production overhead per unit	£2
Opening inventory	800 units
Budgeted fixed production overhead	£9,600 per month
Budgeted production	2,400 units per month
Budgeted sales	2,350 units per month

(a) **Calculate the contribution per unit. You must show all workings**

(2 marks)

(b) Calculate the profit per unit using full absorption costing. You must show all workings.

(2 marks)

(c) Explain ONE advantage to using marginal costing and ONE advantage of using full absorption costing.

(2 marks)

(d) Complete the table below to show the statement of profit or loss under marginal costing and absorption costing principles.

	Marginal costing		Absorption costing	
	£	£	£	£
Sales		44,650		44,650
Less: cost of sales				
Opening inventory			10,400	
Variable production costs	21,600			
Production costs				
Closing inventory			(11,050)	
Cost of sales				
Contribution				
Fixed costs		(9,600)		
Profit				

(4 marks)

(e) **Complete the following sentence.**

[▼] is the required method of inventory costing under IAS 2 *Inventories.* IAS 2 also requires inventories to be measured at the [▼] of cost and [▼] .

(3 marks)

Picklist:

Marginal costing
Absorption costing
higher
lower
carrying amount
net realisable value

....

Task 4 (15 marks)

You are currently working on the year-end financial statements of Sauter. You have contacted Jonas, the accounts assistant at Sauter to get the necessary data about revenue and costs. The files are quite large and Jonas has suggested that you become "friends" on a well-known social media site and he will use the messaging function of that site to transfer and share financial information with you. He has suggested that you should also send any information back to him using this site for convenience.

(a) **Referring to the AAT *Code of Professional Ethics* explain the ethical principles that are at risk here.**

(4 marks)

(b) **What actions should you take to reduce the risks to the ethical principles?**

(2 marks)

Jonas was entering data into the Sauter accounting system, but his computer crashed and the data was deleted and lost. A back-up copy has not been made.

You have receive the following message:

To: Jamie9573

From: Jonas2004

Subject: Missing information

Hi,

I have lost some important financial information. The information I need is amounts paid and received for trade purchases and sales revenue. I need these figures for the year-end statement of profit or loss.

I have been able to recover that opening payables amounted to £5,400 and closing payables were £4,800. Amounts paid from our bank account to our trade suppliers amounted to £108,000.

If it is any help the sales team have informed me that we operate on a 20% mark-up on cost and inventory values were negligible.

Please help me! Jonas

(c) **Reply to Jonas' message explaining the approach that is required and also supply the sales and purchase figures that he is requesting.**

(9 marks)

Task 5 (12 marks)

Jonas has asked you for your help in calculating the total cost for a new one-off job specifically requested by a client. He has provided you with the following information:

	Department A	Department B
Direct materials cost	£800	£1,400
Direct labour: wage rate per hour	£12	£10
Direct labour hours	14	22

The policy of Sauter is to allocate fixed overheads as follows:

- Fixed production overheads – £4 per labour hour
- Fixed administration overheads – 60% of total production cost

Sauter applies a 15% mark-up on cost on one-off jobs.

(a) **Complete the following table. Show your answers to the nearest whole pound.**

	£	£
Direct materials – A		
Direct materials – B		
Direct labour – A		
Direct labour – B		
Fixed production overhead		
Total production cost		

	£	£
Fixed administration overhead		
Total cost		
Profit		
Selling price		

(12 marks)

Task 6 (13 marks)

You have been requested to complete the draft statement of financial position for Sauter as at 31 December 20X7.

Jonas has provided you with the following trial balance at 31 December 20X7:

	Dr £	Cr £
Non-current assets costs	390,000	
Inventory (closing)	86,000	
Sales ledger control	56,000	
Drawings	42,000	
Cash and bank	28,000	
Capital introduced		200,000
Non-current assets accumulated depreciation		167,000
Profit for the year		151,400
Purchase ledger control		62,400
Bank loan		13,500
VAT		6,580
Allowance for doubtful debts		1,120
	602,000	602,000

(a) **Complete the table below to prepare the statement of financial position.**

	£	£
Non-current assets		
Cost		
Accumulated depreciation		
Current assets		
Inventory		
Trade receivables		
Cash and bank		
Total current assets		
Current liabilities		
Trade payables	(62,400)	
VAT	(6,580)	
Total current liabilities		(68,980)
Bank loan		(13,500)
Net current assets		
Financed by:		

(13 marks)

BPP PRACTICE ASSESSMENT 2
LEVEL 3 SYNOPTIC ASSESSMENT

ANSWERS

Advanced Diploma Synoptic Assessment (ADSY) BPP practice assessment 2

Task 1

(a) A professional accountant who complies with the law, brings no disrepute on the profession and is perceived as being ethical by other people has complied with the fundamental principle of ▢ professional behaviour ▢ .

(b)

	✓
Sustainability and CSR are not financial matters and sit outside the remit of the professional accountant.	
Sustainability and CSR form part of the accountant's obligation to work in the public interest.	✓
Sustainability and CSR are key considerations for accountants working in particularly industries, such as the renewable energy industry.	

(c)

Action	✓
Professional negligence	✓
Self interest	
Fraud under false representation	

(d)

Statement	True	False
Due diligence procedures are not necessary as this situation relates to an existing client.		✓
You should report this matter urgently to the relevant authorities. There is clearly something amiss.		✓

(e) As a result of this letter, Piers faces threats of ▢ self-interest ▢ and ▢ intimidation ▢ to his professional ethics.

(f)

Action	Yes/No
Integrity	✓
Objectivity	✓
Confidentiality	
Professional competence and due care	
Professional behaviour	✓

(g)

	✓
Hide the letter back in the in-tray and pretend you never saw it; it would not do for you to get caught up in this mess	
Report the misconduct immediately to the AAT	
Discuss the situation with your immediate line manager	✓

··

Task 2

(a)

Account name	Amount £	Debit ✓	Credit ✓
Non-current assets: vehicles	13,500	✓	
Bank loan	13,500		✓

(b)   £4,000

Working

$$\frac{£13,500 - £1,500}{3 \text{ years}} = £4,000 \text{ per annum}$$

(c)

	✓
Depreciation spreads the cost of an asset over its residual life	✓
All tangible non-current assets must be depreciated	
Depreciation is debited to retained earnings	
Accumulated depreciation reduces the carrying amount of the tangible non-current asset	✓

Tangible non-current assets with an infinite useful life, such as land, are not depreciated.

Depreciation is debited as an expense in the statement of profit or loss.

(d)

Account name	Amount £	Debit ✓	Credit ✓
Irrecoverable debt expense	6,700	✓	
Sales ledger control	6,700		✓

(e)

	✓
The allowance for doubtful debts is an expense in the statement of profit or loss	
The allowance for doubtful debts increases the trade receivables balance	
The allowance for doubtful debts reflects the possible non-payment of some receivable balances	✓

(f) The allowance for doubtful debts will be decreased by £480 .

(g)

	✓
Leave the work on this lease agreement for another colleague to find, after all, Sauter will chase if they haven't heard anything for a while	
Show a willing attitude and give it your best shot	
Consult with your line manager about the task	✓

Consult with your line manager about your concerns about completing the work. If you are still in doubt then ask to be removed from the work. Do not attempt to complete the work if you do not feel you have the knowledge and experience to do so. It would unethical to leave the work you should contact your line manager who will be able to reassign it to someone with the relevant knowledge and experience.

(h)

	✓
Confidentiality	
Professional competence and due care	✓
Objectivity	

Task 3

(a)

	£	£
Selling price per unit		19
Less:		
Direct materials per unit	(4)	
Direct labour per unit	(3)	
Variable production overhead per unit	(2)	
Marginal cost per unit		(9)
Contribution per unit		10

(b)

		£
Selling price per unit		19
Marginal cost per unit	(9)	
Fixed production cost per unit (£96,000 / 24,000 units)	(4)	
Full absorption cost per unit		(13)
Profit per unit		6

(c) Absorption costing allows a manager to see whether all costs are covered by the sales made.

Marginal costing is more useful for making short term production decisions.

(d)

	Marginal costing		Absorption costing	
	£	£	£	£
Sales		44,650		44,650
Less: cost of sales				
Opening inventory	7,200		10,400	
Variable production costs	21,600			
Production costs			31,200	
Closing inventory	(7,650)		(11,050)	
Cost of sales		(21,150)		(30,550)
Contribution		23,500		
Fixed costs		(9,600)		
Profit		13,900		14,100

Marginal costing

- Opening inventory: 800 units × £9 marginal cost per unit = £7,200
- Closing inventory: (800 + 2,400 – 2,350) units × £9 = £7,650

Absorption costing

- Production costs: 2,400 units × £13 = £31,200

(e) | Absorption costing | is the required method of inventory costing under IAS 2 *Inventories*. IAS 2 also requires inventories to be measured at the | lower | of cost and | net realisable value |.

··

Task 4

(a) The two ethical principles most at risk here are confidentiality and professional behaviour.

Organisations have a professional and legal obligation to keep data and information secure and confidential. Typically this will require strict access policies and the use of password protection. Jonas' use of social media to transfer company information is risking a breach of confidentiality and is likely against company policy. In respect of the data protection regulations it is likely to be illegal as well.

The second principle at risk here is professional behaviour. It were to be public knowledge that Sauter or Broadchurch & Co was using this method of transferring sensitive information this would bring disrepute to the companies and the accountancy profession.

(b) I must refuse to share and exchange information in this way and only communicate information as per company policies on information and data. I should also report this matter to my supervisor as this is a serious breach of company policy and can have wider legal implications and affect respect for the accountancy profession.

(c) To: Jonas@Sauter

From: Jamie@Broadchurch

Subject: Missing information

Jonas

Firstly I must remind you that Sauter has a responsibility to keep proper books of accounts that would be able to supply this information.

However, when there are incomplete records we can use various techniques to reconstruct the missing information from the records we do have. Incomplete records can occur when proper records have not been kept or in unusual circumstances through fire, flood or system crashes.

Amounts that are missing can be reconstructed by the use of raw data, for example paying-in stubs, bank statements, invoices and credit notes. When opening and closing balances are known balancing figures can sometimes be inserted into workings to discover missing amounts. Other methods can include the use of percentage mark-ups and margins to calculate missing figures. This can include the reconstruction of sales revenue, cost of sales and gross profit figures.

Trade purchases

The bank statement shows that £108,000 has actually been paid to trade suppliers however this has to be adjusted for the opening and closing balances to show how much should go into the statement of profit or loss. This is part of the matching or accruals concept.

£108,000 plus amounts outstanding at the end of the year = £108,000 + £4,800 = £112,800 less £5,400 that relates to the previous year = £112,800 – £5,400 = £107,400

£107,400 is the amount to be included in the statement of profit or loss for trade purchases.

Sales revenue

As we operate on a 20% plus cost basis sales revenue is £107,400 × 1.20 = £128,880.

I hope that helps.

Regards,

Jamie

Broadchurch & Co

....

Task 5

(a)

		£	£
Direct materials – A		£800	
Direct materials – B		£1,400	
Direct labour – A	£12 × 14 hours	£168	
Direct labour – B	£10 × 22 hours	£220	
Fixed production overhead	£4 × (14 + 22) hours	£144	
Total production cost			£2,732
Fixed administration overhead	60% × £2,732		£1,639
Total cost			£4,371
Profit	£4,371 × 15%		£656
Selling price			£5,027

....

Task 6

	£	£
Non-current assets		
Cost	390,000	
Accumulated depreciation	(167,000)	
		223,000
Current assets		
Inventory	86,000	
Trade receivables	54,880	
Cash and bank	28,000	
Total current assets		168,880
Current liabilities		
Trade payables	(62,400)	
VAT	(6,580)	
Total current liabilities		(68,980)
Bank loan		(13,500)
Net current assets		309,400
Financed by:		
Capital introduced	200,000	
Profit for the year	151,400	
Less: drawings	(42,000)	
Closing capital		309,400
Total capital and liabilities		391,880

Workings:

- NCA: 390k – 167k = 223k

- Receivables: Sales ledger control – allowance for doubtful debts = £56,000 – £1,120 = £54,880

BPP PRACTICE ASSESSMENT 3
LEVEL 3 SYNOPTIC ASSESSMENT

Time allowed: 2 hours and 30 minutes

PRACTICE ASSESSMENT 3

Advanced Diploma Synoptic Assessment (ADSY)
BPP practice assessment 3

Task 1 is based on a workplace scenario separate to the rest of the assessment.

Task 2 to **Task 6** is based on the workplace scenario of Kasablanka which is as follows:

> You are Ally, a part-qualified accounting technician. You work on all aspects of bookkeeping and accounting for Kasablanka, a manufacturing business. Kasablanka is owned and run by Gleb Savko.
>
> Kasablanka uses the services of Dander & Co, a firm of accountants.

Task 1 (15 marks)

Rose Well is a sole practitioner accountant who has a client, Baxter Links. She has evidence that Baxter has been selling counterfeit goods. She decides that she will discuss this with him at their next meeting.

(a) **Which of the following statements is true or false about the action Rose proposes to take in this matter?**

Statement	True	False
Rose may be guilty of the crime of tipping off a client		
Rose will be guilty of breaching confidentiality if she reports Baxter without discussing her suspicions with him first		
Rose should report her findings to her nominated officer prior to talking to Baxter		

(3 marks)

(b) **Complete the following statement.**

The FRC aims to promote ethical [▼] and increased [▼] in the accountancy profession in the UK.

Picklist:

accounting
compliance
confidence
financial reporting
practices

(2 marks)

(c) **Are these statements true or false?**

Statement	True	False
The need to act ethically is most important for accountants employed in the public sector as they are more open to criticism if this money is perceived to be spent inappropriately.		
The *Code of Professional Ethics* sets out the required standards of professional behaviour with guidance on how these standards can be achieved.		
The *Code of Professional Ethics* adopts a principles-based approach in order to allow individuals to choose appropriate behaviour and to remove the need for professional judgements to be made.		

(3 marks)

You have recently terminated your relationship with a client after discovering a number of errors in their VAT return that they refused to correct.

(d) **You withdrew from this engagement to safeguard against which threat to your fundamental principles?**

	✓
Familiarity	
Self-interest	
Intimidation	

(2 marks)

You have now been approached by the client's new accountant who has asked you why the agreement ended.

(e) **Which of the fundamental principles does this threaten?**

	✓
Professional behaviour	
Confidentiality	
Objectivity	

(1 mark)

You have just found out that, as result of the discovery of previously withheld information, the financial statements of a client are materially misstated. Several months ago you issued an audit report which confirmed that the statements presented a true and fair view.

(f) **Which of the below statements are true?**

Statement	✓
You failed to comply with the ethical principle of professional competence and due care at the time of the audit.	
You failed to comply with the ethical principle of integrity at the time of the audit.	
You complied with the ethical principles at the time of the audit.	

(2 marks)

(g) **Which of the following actions should now be taken?**

Action	✓
You should make a note on the audit file for next year. The report on these financial statements has already been issued and it is too late to retract it.	
You should issue a revised audit report immediately.	
You should securely destroy the new information to prevent damage to your reputation as a professional accountant.	

(2 marks)

Task 2 (12 marks)

You have found an error in the payroll information recently sent to HMRC. You are concerned that this may breach legislation, so you consider consulting a technical helpline set up by a local accountancy firm to determine what you should do next.

(a) **According to the ethical code, which of your fundamental principles would be under threat if you called the helpline?**

Integrity ☐

Confidentiality ☐

Objectivity ☐

(1 mark)

In May 20X8, Kasablanka purchased a new forklift truck at a cost of £25,000. The accounting policy is to depreciate such assets over 5 years on a straight line basis with a full year of depreciation recorded in the year of acquisition and none in the year of disposal. The scrap value of the asset is estimated to be £2,500. Costs of £250 were incurred in the delivery and set up of the forklift truck.

(b) **Calculate the depreciation charge for the forklift truck for the year ended 31 December 20X8.**

£ [   ]

(2 marks)

(c) **What is the carrying amount of the asset at 31 December 20X8?**

£ [   ]

(1 mark)

(d) **Select which ONE of the following statements is an ADVANTAGE of using the FIFO method when determining the cost of inventory by ticking in the relevant box.**

Reason	✓
Inventory is valued at a price which most closely represents the current market value.	
It complies with IAS 2 *Accounting for Inventory*.	
It is easy to calculate when there is a high volume of stock movement in and out of the business.	
Fluctuations in prices are smoothed out, making it easier to analyse the data for decision making.	

(2 marks)

(e) **You have been asked to calculate the allowance for doubtful debts. Which ONE of the following statements is correct?**

	✓
The allowance for doubtful debts must be based on Kasablanka's accounting policy which takes 15% of the value held at the year-end on the trade receivable account	
The allowance should be based on specifically identified customer debts which are expected to be irrecoverable	
The allowance should be adjusted to ensure the correct level of profit for Kasablanka at year end	

(1 mark)

(f) **Select which of the following statements are true or false regarding sole traders and limited companies.**

	True ✓	False ✓
Limited companies are separate legal entities from the shareholders.		
Directors can have a 'drawings' account like a sole trader.		
Financial statements must always be prepared in accordance with recognised accounting standards. This is correct for both sole traders and limited companies.		
The Companies Act 2006 states that the directors of a limited company must file annual accounts.		
Only large companies may use International Financial Reporting Standards as the basis for their financial statements preparation.		

(5 marks)

Task 3 (13 marks)

Gleb intends to purchase a new piece of production machinery. He has narrowed the selection to two machines, both of which cost £80,000.

Details about the two machines are as follows:

	Machine 1	Machine 2
Cost	£80,000	£80,000
Expected useful life	4 years	5 years
Scrap value	£8,000	Nil

Kasablanka charges depreciation annually on a straight-line over the expected useful life of an asset, with a full year charge in the year of acquisition and none in the year of disposal.

(a) **Calculate the depreciation per annum for machine 1 and machine 2. You must show your workings.**

(4 marks)

(b) **Complete the table below to calculate the net present value for each machine.**

	Discount factor	Machine 1 cash flow	Discounted cashflow	Machine 2 cash flow	Discounted cash flow
	8%	£	£	£	£
Year 0	1.000	(80,000)	(80,000)	(80,000)	(80,000)
Year 1	0.926	20,000	18,520	18,000	16,668
Year 2	0.857	25,000		18,000	15,426
Year 3	0.794	29,000	23,026	25,000	
Year 4	0.735	29,000	21,315	25,000	18,375
Year 5	0.681			25,000	17,025
NPV					

(4 marks)

(c)   Complete the following sentence.

When considering the net present values of the two machines, Gleb would

be better to choose the machine with a [▼   ] net present value.

Picklist:

higher

lower

(1 mark)

(d)   Explain TWO advantages and TWO disadvantages of the net present value method.

(4 marks)

Task 4 (15 marks)

Kasablanka Ltd has a year end of 31 December 20X8

It is just after the year-end and you are currently working on the inventory value to go into the extended trial balance. For many years Kasablanka has used a weighted average cost (AVCO) method in the calculation of inventory values but this year one of the directors has requested you to use a 'last in first out' (LIFO) method. The reason given for this was that purchase costs increased considerably towards the end of the year so this would reflect 'economic reality' and we can change back to AVCO next year when costs have settled down to a more normal level. Kasablanka is keen to keep their corporation tax at a minimum this financial year. The director also mentioned that he is in the process of considering the approval of your annual leave request.

(a)   Identify and explain the ethical principles at risk here along with any associated threats to those principles.

(6 marks)

(b)   What actions should you take in these circumstances?

(5 marks)

Bill is a new manager of Kasablanka and he used to run a small vegetable stall as a sole trader. He is struggling to understand why the financial statements 'are so complex'.

(c)   Explain to Bill what is the purpose of financial statements, and briefly discuss how the results of the business are reported. Consider who is likely to use the accounts.

(4 marks)

Task 5 (12 marks)

Gleb Savko has asked you to carry out an analysis of the company's overheads for products AB and CD because he is not satisfied with the accuracy of the current absorption basis used, which is labour hours.

	AB £	CD £
Overhead absorption rate per labour hour	107	27

He wants to see the results of using machine hours to absorb overheads, and using activity-based costing (ABC) to calculate absorbed overheads. The information relating to the next accounting period that you need to carry out this analysis is attached.

	AB	CD
Number of machine hours per unit	7	3
Production set-ups	4	7
Number of units	100	500
Orders executed	4	32

	£
Production set up costs	5,000
Quality control	13,500
Materials handling and despatch	5,500
Total overheads	24,000

(a) **Complete the following table and calculate the overhead absorption rate per machine hour. You should round to the nearest £.**

		AB	CD	Total
	£	£	£	£
Total machine hours				
Overhead absorption rate				
Overhead absorption rate per machine hour				

(4 marks)

(b) **Complete the following table and calculate the overhead absorption rate using ABC. You should round to the nearest £.**

	Cost per driver £	AB	CD	Total
Set-ups		4	7	11
Cost per set-up				
Set-up costs				
Number of units		100	500	600
Quality control cost per unit produced				
Quality control costs				
Orders executed		4	32	36
Materials handling and despatch cost per order executed				
Materials handling and despatch costs				
Total overheads absorbed				
Overheads absorbed per unit				

(8 marks)

Task 6 (13 marks)

You are in the process of preparing the final accounts for Kasablanka for the year ended 31 December 20X8.

The trial balance is as follows:

	£	£
Bank	4,750	
Capital		20,000
Closing inventory	2,760	2,760
Non-current assets at cost	125,000	
Accumulated depreciation		17,500
Depreciation charge	2,500	
Long term loan		7,500
General expenses	56,260	
Opening inventory	3,000	
Trade payables		2,320
Trade receivables	1,950	
Sales		303,405
Purchases	155,770	
Suspense	1,495	
	353,485	**353,485**

Further information is available:

- Prepayments of £1,120 were credited to the general expenses account in the SPL, however, the other side of the entry was not entered.

- An accrual for general expenses of £520 needs to be accounted for at year end.

- Interest paid of £375 was credited from the bank and cash account, but no expense was entered in the general ledger.

(a) **Clear the suspense account and enter the adjustments required in the adjustments columns.**

	Ledger balances		Adjustments	
	£	£	£	£
Bank	4,750			
Capital		20,000		
Closing inventory	2,760	2,760		
Non-current assets at cost	125,000			
Accumulated depreciation		17,500		
Depreciation charge	2,500			
Long term loan		7,500		
General expenses	56,260			
Interest paid				
Opening inventory	3,000			
Prepayments				
Accruals				
Trade payables		2,320		
Trade receivables	1,950			
Sales		303,405		
Purchases	155,770			
Suspense	1,495			
	353,485	**353,485**	**2,015**	**2,015**

(5 marks)

(b) **Use the adjusted trial balance to complete the statement of profit or loss.**

Kasablanca

Statement of profit or loss for the year ended 31 December 20X8

	£	£
Sales		303,405
Cost of sales:		
Opening inventory	3,000	
Purchases		
Closing inventory		
Gross profit		
Less:		
General expenses		
Depreciation charge	2,500	
Profit before interest and tax		
Interest paid		(375)
Profit for the year		

(8 marks)

BPP PRACTICE ASSESSMENT 3
LEVEL 3 SYNOPTIC ASSESSMENT

ANSWERS

Advanced Diploma Synoptic Assessment (ADSY)
BPP practice assessment 3

Task 1

(a)

Statement	True	False
Rose may be guilty of the crime of tipping off a client	✓	
Rose will be guilty of breaching confidentiality if she reports Baxter without discussing her suspicions with him first		✓
Rose should report her findings to her Nominated Officer prior to talking to Baxter		✓

Rose may be guilty of 'tipping off' the client if she takes any action which may be deemed to prejudice an investigation – such as discussing her evidence with him in advance of notifying the NCA.

As she has specific knowledge and reasonable grounds to suspect money laundering is taking place, she will be legally allowed to breach confidentiality in this instance under the The Money Laundering, Terrorist Financing and Transfer of Funds (Information on the Payer) Regulations 2017. Rose will have a professional duty to report it.

As Rose is a sole practitioner, she will not have a Nominated Officer. Instead, she will have to consider making a report direct to the NCA.

(b) The FRC aims to promote ethical | financial reporting | and increased

| confidence | in the accountancy profession in the UK.

(c)

Statement	True	False
The need to act ethically is most important for accountants employed in the public sector as they are more open to criticism if this money is perceived to be spent inappropriately.		✓
The *Code of Professional Ethics* sets out the required standards of professional behaviour with guidance on how these standards can be achieved.	✓	
The *Code of Professional Ethics* adopts a principles-based approach in order to allow individuals to choose appropriate behaviour and to remove the need for professional judgements to be made.		✓

(d)

	✓
Familiarity	
Self-interest	
Intimidation	✓

(e)

	✓
Professional behaviour	
Confidentiality	✓
Objectivity	

(f)

	✓
You failed to comply with the ethical principle of professional competence and due care at the time of the audit.	
You failed to comply with the ethical principle of integrity at the time of the audit.	
You complied with the ethical principles at the time of the audit.	✓

(g)

	✓
You should make a note on the audit file for next year. The report on these financial statements has already been issued and it is too late to retract it.	
You should issue a revised audit report immediately.	✓
You should securely destroy the new information to prevent damage to your reputation as a professional accountant.	

Task 2

(a)

Integrity ☐

Confidentiality ☑

Objectivity ☐

(b)

£	4,550

Workings

	£
Cost	25,000
Add delivery costs	250
Less scrap value	(2,500)
Amount to be depreciated over 5 years	22,750
Charge for the year	4,550

(c)

£	20,700

Workings: £25,250 – £4,550

(d)

Reason	✓
Inventory issued is valued at a price which most closely represents the current market value.	
It complies with IAS 2 *Accounting for Inventory*.	✓
It is easy to calculate when there is a high volume of stock movement in and out of the business.	
Fluctuations in prices are smoothed out, making it easier to analyse the data for decision making.	

Option 1 is a benefit of LIFO. Option 3 and option 4 are benefits of the weighted average cost valuation method.

(e)

	✓
The allowance for doubtful debts must be based on Kasablanka's accounting policy which takes 15% of the value held at the year-end on the trade receivable account	
The allowance should be based on the specifically identified customer debts which are expected to be irrecoverable	✓
The allowance should be adjusted to ensure the correct level of profit for Kasablanka at year end	

Allowances for doubtful debts can either be based on specifically identified debts which are expected to be irrecoverable at the year end, or a general allowance based on past experience. They should be based on factual evidence and the best estimation of whether they are really recoverable.

They should not be used to alter the profit required.

(f)

	True	False
Limited companies are separate legal entities from the shareholders.	✓	
Directors can have a 'drawings' account like a sole trader.		✓
Financial statements must always be prepared in accordance with recognised accounting standards. This is correct for both sole traders and limited companies.		✓
The Companies Act 2006 states that the directors of a limited company must file annual accounts.	✓	
Only large companies may use International Financial Reporting Standards as the basis for their financial statements preparation.		✓

Task 3

(a)

	Machine 1 £	Machine 2 £
Cost	80,000	80,000
Residual value	8,000	0
	72,000	80,000
Expected useful life (years)	4	5
Annual depreciation charge	18000	16000

(b)

	Discount factor 8%	Machine 1 cash flow £	Discounted cashflow £	Machine 2 cash flow £	Discounted cash flow £
Year 0	1.000	(80,000)	(80,000)	(80,000)	(80,000)
Year 1	0.926	20,000	18,520	18,000	16,668
Year 2	0.857	25,000	21,425	18,000	15,426
Year 3	0.794	29,000	23,026	25,000	19,850
Year 4	0.735	29,000	21,315	25,000	18,375
Year 5	0.681			25,000	17,025
NPV			4,286		7,344

(c) When considering the net present values of the two machines, Gleb would be better to choose the machine with a [higher] net present value.

(d) Note: only two advantages and two disadvantages were required.

NPV advantages

- NPV accounts for the time value of money by giving weight to earlier cash flows

- It is consistent with the objective of maximising shareholders' wealth as the project with the most positive NPV should be accepted

- It is based on cashflows which are less subjective than profits

- it is a simple way to compare projects with different levels of investment, cashflows and timeframe

NPV disadvantages

- identifying an appropriate discount rate can be difficult
- it doesn't consider the risk of a project
- it can be a tricky concept for some to understand

Task 4

(a) The ethical principles at risk can include objectivity and integrity. The financial statements should be prepared without bias or any undue influence. It would be unfair to change the valuation method for one year as this would be against the accounting concept of consistency in the use of accounting policies. Intentionally changing the inventory method for this purpose would be dishonest and in breach of the integrity principle. The threats here are intimidation through the possible refusal of my annual leave request and also a self-interest threat for the director in manipulating profits to minimise tax. An added issue here is that the LIFO method is not allowed for inventory valuation under IAS 2.

(b) It can be possible to change accounting policies provided that there is a valid reason for doing so, for example a change in how an industry is regulated or if it was found that the current policies did not provide a fair reflection of the results of a business. In this case, it appears the only reason is to manipulate profits on a short-term basis, and not following guidance in the accounting standards (IAS 2, Inventories and the Conceptual Framework's principles. therefore I should refer this matter onto my immediate supervisor for authorisation to make this change in the valuation method. When I contact my supervisor I should also mention the impact the change will make on reported profits and also that LIFO is not considered an appropriate valuation method.

(c) The purpose of the financial statements is to show the financial performance of the business during the reporting period. This is reported through the statement of profit or loss. The financial statements will also show the financial status of the business through the statement of financial position. This statement shows the assets and liabilities of the business including the capital invested into the business by its owner or owners as in the case of a partnership.

The financial statements can be used by a variety of users and these can include; employees, customers, suppliers, potential investors, banks and also the tax authorities.

Task 5

(a)

	£	AB £	CD £	Total £
Total machine hours		700	1,500	2,200
Overhead absorption rate	11			
Overhead absorption rate per machine hour		77	33	

(b)

	Cost per driver £	AB	CD	Total
Production set-ups		4	7	11
Cost per set-up (£5,000 / 11)	455			
Production set-up costs		£1,820	£3,185	
Number of units		100	500	600
Quality control cost per unit produced (£13,500 / 600)	23			
Quality control costs		£2,300	£11,500	
Orders executed		4	32	36
Materials handling and despatch cost per order executed (£5,500 / 36)	153			
Materials handling and despatch costs		£612	£4,896	
Total overheads absorbed		£4,732	£19,581	
Overheads absorbed per unit		£47	£39	

Task 6

(a)

	Ledger balances		Adjustments	
	£	£	£	£
Bank	4,750			
Capital		20,000		
Closing inventory	2,760	2,760		
Non-current assets at cost	125,000			
Accumulated depreciation		17,500		
Depreciation charge	2,500			
Long term loan		7,500		
General expenses	56,260		520	
Interest paid			375	
Opening inventory	3,000			
Prepayments			1,120	
Accruals				520
Trade payables		2,320		
Trade receivables	1,950			
Sales		303,405		
Purchases	155,770			
Suspense	1,495			1,495
	353,485	**353,485**	**2,015**	**2,015**

(b)

	£	£
Sales		303,405
Cost of sales:		
Opening inventory	3,000	
Purchases	155,770	
Closing inventory	(2,760)	
		(156,010)
Gross profit		147,395
Less:		
General expenses (56,260 + 520)	56,780	
Depreciation charge	2,500	
		(59,280)
Profit before interest and tax		88,115
Interest paid		(375)
Profit for the year		87,740

Appendix: Reference materials for the synoptic assessment

The information in this section is for use alongside the AAT's sample assessment and the practice assessments in this Question Bank.

This will be available to you in the assessment in pop-up windows.

Code of Professional Ethics (2017)

Code of Professional Ethics – Part A

Introduction – 100

Section 100 – Introduction and code of fundamental principles

100.1   A distinguishing mark of the accountancy profession is its acceptance of the responsibility to act in the public interest. Therefore, your responsibility as a member is not exclusively to satisfy the needs of an individual client or employer. In acting in the public interest, members shall observe and comply with the *Code* of ethical requirements set out in this *Code*.

100.2   This *Code* is in three parts. Part A establishes the code of fundamental principles of professional ethics for members and provides a conceptual framework for applying those principles. The conceptual framework provides guidance on fundamental ethical principles. Members are required to apply this conceptual framework to enable them to identify threats to compliance with the fundamental principles, to evaluate their significance and, if such threats are not clearly insignificant, to apply safeguards to eliminate them or reduce them to an acceptable level such that compliance with the fundamental principles is not compromised.

100.3   Part B and C describe how the conceptual framework applies in certain situations. They provide examples of safeguards that may be appropriate to address threats to compliance with the fundamental principles. They also describe situations where safeguards are not available to address the threats and where the activity or relationship creating the threats shall be avoided. Part B applies to Licensed members. Part C applies to members in business. Licensed members may also find Part C relevant to their particular circumstances.

100.4   In this *Code* the use of the word 'shall' imposes a requirement on the member to comply with the specific provision in which 'shall' has been used. Compliance is required unless an exception is permitted by this *Code*.

Fundamental principles

100.5 A member shall comply with the following fundamentals principles:

(i) **Integrity**: to be straightforward and honest in all professional and business relationships.

(ii) **Objectivity**: to not allow bias, conflict of interest or undue influence of others to override professional or business judgements.

(iii) **Professional competence and due care**: to maintain professional knowledge and skill at the level required to ensure that a client or employer receives competent professional service based on current developments in practice, legislation and techniques. A member shall act diligently and in accordance with applicable technical and professional standards when providing professional services.

(iv) **Confidentiality**: to act, in accordance with the law, respect the confidentiality of information acquired as a result of professional and business relationships and not disclose any such information to third parties without proper and specific authority unless there is legal or professional right or duty to disclose. Confidential information acquired as a result of professional and business relationships shall not be used for the personal advantage of the member or third parties.

(v) **Professional behaviour**: to comply with the relevant laws and regulation and avoid any action that discredits our profession.

Each of these fundamentals principles is discussed in more detail in Sections 110–150.

Conceptual framework approach

100.6 The circumstances in which members operate may give rise to specific threats to compliance with the fundamental principles. It is impossible to define every situation that create such threats and specify the appropriate mitigating action. In addition, the nature of engagements and work assignments may differ and consequently different threats may exist, requiring the application of different safeguards. Therefore, this *Code* establishes a conceptual framework that requires a member to identify, evaluate and address threats to compliance with the fundamental principles. The conceptual framework approach assists members in complying with the ethical requirements of this *Code* and meeting their responsibility to act in the public interest. It accommodates many variations in circumstances that create threats to compliance with the fundamental principles and can deter a professional accountant from concluding that a situation is permitted if it is not specifically prohibited.

100.7 When a member identifies threats to compliance with the fundamental principles and, based on an evaluation of those threats, determines that they are not at an acceptable level, the member shall determine whether appropriate safeguards are available and can be applied to eliminate the threats or reduce them to an acceptable level. In making that determination, the member shall exercise professional judgement and take into account whether a reasonable and informed third party, weighing all the specific facts and circumstances available to the member at the time, would be likely to conclude that the threats would be eliminated or reduced to an acceptable level by the application of the safeguards, such that compliance with the fundamental principles is not compromised.

100.8 A member shall evaluate any threats to compliance with the fundamental principles when the member knows, or could reasonably be expected to know, of circumstances or relationships that may compromise compliance with the fundamental principles.

100.9 A member shall take qualitative as well as quantitative factors into account when considering the significance of a threat. When applying the conceptual framework, a member may encounter situations in which threats cannot be eliminated or reduced to an acceptable level, either because the threat is too significant or because appropriate safeguards are not available, or cannot be applied. In such situations, a member shall decline or discontinue the specific professional service involved or, when necessary, resign from the engagement (in the case of a Licensed member) or the employing organisation (in the case of a member in business).

100.10 Sections 290 and 291 (as detailed within the associated document *Code of Professional Ethics: independence provisions relating to review and assurance engagements*) contain provisions with which a member shall comply if the member identifies a breach of an independence provision of the *Code*. If a member identifies a breach of any other provisions of this *Code*, the member shall evaluate the significance of the breach and its impact on the member's ability to comply with the fundamental principles. The member shall take whatever actions that may be available, as soon as possible, to satisfactorily address the consequences of the breach. The member shall determine whether to report the breach, for example, to those who may have been affected by the breach, a member body, relevant regulator or oversight authority.

100.11 When a member encounters unusual circumstances in which the application of a specific requirement of the *Code* would result in a disproportionate outcome or an outcome that may not be in public interest, it is recommended that the member consult with AAT on the issue.

Threats and safeguards

100.12 Threats may be created by a broad range of relationships and circumstances. When a relationship or circumstance creates a threat, such a threat could compromise, or could be perceived to compromise, a member's compliance with the fundamental principles. A circumstance may create more than one threat, and a threat may affect compliance with more than one fundamental principle.

Threats fall into the following categories:

(i) self-interest threats, which may occur where a financial or other investment will inappropriately influence the member's judgement or behaviour

(ii) self-review threats, which may occur when a previous judgement needs to be re-evaluated by the member responsible for that judgement

(iii) advocacy threats, which may occur when a member promotes a position or opinion to the point that subsequent objectivity may be compromised

(iv) familiarity threats, which may occur when, because of a close or personal relationship, a member becomes too sympathetic to the interests of others

(v) intimidation threats, which may occur when a member may be deterred from acting objectively by threats, whether actual or perceived.

Parts B and C of this *Code* explain how these categories of threats may be created for Licensed members and members in business respectively. Licensed members may also find Part C relevant to their particular circumstances.

100.13 Safeguards are actions or other measures that may eliminate threats or reduce them to an acceptable level. These fall into two broad categories:

(i) safeguards created by the profession, legislation or regulation
(ii) safeguards in the work environment.

100.14 Safeguards created by the profession, legislation or regulation include, but are not restricted to:

(i) educational, training and experience requirements for entry into the profession

(ii) continuing professional development requirements

(iii) corporate governance regulations

(iv) professional standards

(v)   professional or regulatory monitoring and disciplinary procedures

(vi)   external review of the reports, returns, communications or information produced by a member and carried out by a legally empowered third party.

100.15 Parts B and C of this *Code*, respectively, discuss safeguards in the work environment for Licensed members and members in business.

100.16 Certain safeguards may increase the likelihood of identifying or deterring unethical behaviour. Such safeguards, which may be created by the accounting profession, legislation, regulation or an employing organisation, include, but are not restricted to:

(i)   effective, well publicised complaints systems operated by the employing organisation, the profession or a regulator, which enable colleagues, employers and members of the public to draw attention to unprofessional or unethical behaviour

(ii)   an explicitly stated duty to report breaches of ethical requirements.

Conflicts of interest

100.17 A member may be faced with a conflict of interest when undertaking a professional activity. A conflict of interest creates a threat to objectivity and may create threats to the other fundamental principles. Such threats may be created when:

(i)   the member undertakes a professional activity related to a particular matter for two or more parties whose interests with respect to that matter are in conflict; or

(ii)   the interest of the member with respect to a particular matter and the interests of a party for whom the member undertakes a professional activity related to that matter are in conflict.

100.18 Parts B and C of this *Code* discuss conflicts of interest for Licensed members and members in business respectively.

100.19 In evaluating compliance with the fundamental principles, a member may be required to resolve conflict in the application of fundamental principles.

100.20 When initiating either a formal or informal conflict resolution process, a member shall consider the following, either individually or together with others, as part of the resolution process:

- relevant facts
- ethical issues involved
- fundamental principles related to the matter in question
- established internal procedures
- alternative courses of action.

Having considered these factors, a member shall determine the appropriate course of action that is consistent with the fundamental principles identified. The member shall also weigh the consequences of each possible course of action. If the matter remains unresolved, the member may wish to consult with other appropriate persons within the firm or employing organisation for help in obtaining resolution.

100.21 Where a matter involves a conflict with, or within, an organisation, a member shall determine whether to consult with those charged with governance of the organisation, such as the board of directors or the audit committee.

100.22 It may be in the best interests of the member to document the substance of the issue and details of any discussions held or decisions taken concerning that issue.

100.23 If a significant conflict cannot be resolved, a member may consider obtaining professional advice from the relevant professional body or legal advisers on a confidential basis and thereby obtain guidance on ethical issues without breaching confidentiality. For example, a member may suspect that he or she has encountered a fraud and may need to discuss confidential information in order to satisfy themselves as to whether their suspicions are justified. In such circumstances, the member shall also consider the requirement under the anti-money laundering legislation to submit a report to NCA or to the firm's Money Laundering Reporting Officer (MLRO).

100.24 If, after exhausting all relevant possibilities, the ethical conflict remains unresolved, a member shall, where possible, refuse to remain associated with the matter creating the conflict. The member shall determine whether, in the circumstances, it is appropriate to withdraw from the engagement team or specific assignment, or to resign altogether from the engagement, the firm or the employing organisation.

Integrity

Section 110 – Integrity

110.1 The principle of integrity imposes an obligation on all members to be straightforward and honest in professional and business relationships. Integrity also implies fair dealing and truthfulness.

110.2 A member shall not be associated with reports, returns, communications or other information where they believe that the information:

- contains a false or misleading statement

- contains statements or information furnished recklessly

- omits or obscures information required to be included where such omission or obscurity would be misleading.

When a member becomes aware that they have been associated with such information they shall take steps to be disassociated from the information.

110.3   A member will not be considered to be in breach of paragraph 110.2 if the member provides a modified report in respect of a matter contained in paragraph 110.2.

Section 120 – Objectivity

120.1   The principle of objectivity imposes an obligation on all members not to compromise their professional or business judgement because of bias, conflict of interest or the undue influence of others.

120.2   A member may be exposed to situations that may impair objectivity. It is impractical to define and prescribed all such situations. Relationships that bias or unduly influence the professional judgement of the member shall be avoided. A member shall not perform a professional service if a circumstance or relationship biases or unduly influences their professional judgement with respect to that service.

Section 130 – Professional competence and due care

130.1   The principle of professional competence and due care imposes the following obligations on members:

- to maintain professional knowledge and skill at the level required to ensure that clients or employers receive competent professional service and

- to act diligently in accordance with applicable technical and professional standards when providing professional services.

130.2   Competent professional service requires the exercise of sound judgement in applying professional knowledge and skills in the performance of such service. Professional competence may be divided into two separate phrases:

- attainment of professional competence and
- maintenance of professional competence.

130.3   The maintenance of professional competence requires continuing awareness and understanding of relevant technical, professional and business developments. Continuing professional development (CPD) develops and maintains the capabilities that enable a member to perform competently within the professional environment. To achieve this, the Council expects all members to undertake CPD in accordance with the *AAT Policy on Continuing Professional Development*. This requires members to assess, plan, action and evaluate their learning and development needs. Licensed members should also refer to paragraph 200.3.

130.4 Diligence encompasses the responsibility to act in accordance with the requirements of an assignment, carefully thoroughly and on a timely basis.

130.5 A member shall take reasonable steps to ensure that those working under the member's authority in a professional capacity have appropriate training and supervision.

130.6 Where appropriate, a member shall make clients, employers or other users of the professional services aware of limitations inherent in the services to avoid the misinterpretation of an expression of opinion as an assertion of fact.

Section 140 – Confidentiality

In general terms, there is a legal obligation to maintain the confidentiality of information which is given or obtained in circumstances giving rise to a duty of confidentiality. There are some situations where the law allows a breach of this duty.

The following sections help to explain what this means in practice for members as well as giving guidance on the standards required of members from an ethical perspective.

140.1 The principle of confidentiality imposes an obligation on members to refrain from:

- disclosing outside the firm or employing organisation confidential information acquired as a result of professional and business relationships without proper and specific authority or unless there is a legal or professional right or duty to disclose and

- using confidential information acquired as a result of professional and business relationships to their personal advantage or the advantage of third parties.

Information about a past, present, or prospective client's or employer's affairs, or the affairs of clients of employers, acquired in a work context, is likely to be confidential if it is not a matter of public knowledge.

140.2 A member shall maintain confidentiality even in a social environment. The member shall be alert to the possibility of inadvertent disclosure, particularly in circumstances involving close or personal relations, associates and long established business relationships.

140.3 A member shall maintain confidentiality of information disclosed by a prospective client or employer.

140.4 A member shall maintain confidentiality of information within the firm or employing organisation.

140.5   A member shall take all reasonable steps to ensure that staff under their control and persons from whom advice and assistance is obtained respect the principle of confidentiality. The restriction on using confidential information also means not using it for any purpose other than that for which it was legitimately acquired.

140.6   The need to comply with the principle of confidentiality continues even after the end of relationships between a member and a client or employer. When a member changes employment or acquires a new client, the member is entitled to use prior experience. The member shall not, however, use or disclose any confidential information either acquired or received as a result of a professional or business relationship.

140.7   As a fundamental principle, confidentiality serves the public interest because it facilitates the free flow of information from the client to the member. Nevertheless, the following are circumstances where a member may be required to disclose confidential information or when such disclosure may be appropriate:

- where disclosure is permitted by law and is authorised by the client or the employer (or any other person to whom an obligation of confidence is owed) for example:

    - production of documents or other provision of evidence in the course of legal proceedings or

    - disclosure to the appropriate public authorities (for example, HMRC) of infringements of the law that come to light

    - disclosure of actual or suspected money laundering or terrorist financing to the member's firm's MLRO or to NCA if the member is a sole practitioner, or

- where there is a professional duty or right to disclose, which is in the public interest, and is not prohibited by law. Examples may include:

    - to comply with the quality review of an IFAC member body or other relevant professional body

    - to respond to an inquiry or investigation by AAT or relevant regulatory or professional body

    - to protect the member's professional interests in legal proceedings

    - to comply with technical standards and ethics requirements.

This is a difficult and complex area and members are therefore specifically advised to seek professional advice before disclosing confidential information under c above.

140.8 In deciding whether to disclose confidential information, members should consider the following points:

- whether the interest of all parties, including third parties, could be harmed even though the client or employer (or other person to whom there is a duty of confidentiality) consents to the disclosure of information by the member

- whether all the relevant information is known and substantiated, to the extent that this is practicable. When the situation involves unsubstantiated facts, incomplete information or unsubstantiated conclusions, professional judgement should be used in determining the type of disclosure to be made, if any

- the type of communication or disclosure that may be made and by whom it is to be received; in particular, members should be satisfied that the parties to whom the communication is addressed are appropriate recipients.

Members who are in any doubt about their obligations in a particular situation should seek professional advice.

Section 150 – Professional behaviour

150.1 The principle of professional behaviour imposes an obligation on members to comply with relevant laws and regulations and avoid any action that may bring disrepute to the profession. This includes actions which a reasonable and informed third party, having knowledge of all relevant information, would conclude negatively affect the good reputation of the profession.

Members should note that conduct reflecting adversely on the reputation of AAT is a ground for disciplinary action under *AAT's Disciplinary Regulations.*

150.2 An example of this principle is that in marketing and promoting themselves and their work, members shall be honest and truthful. They may bring the profession into disrepute if they:

- make exaggerated claims for the services they are able to offer, the qualifications they possess, or experience they have gained

- make disparaging references or unsubstantiated comparison to the work of others.

Section 160 – Taxation

160.1 Members performing taxation services in the UK, Ireland and in other member states of the EU will be dealing with compliance and advice on direct and indirect taxes based on income, gains, losses and profits. The administrative authorities and the legal basis for direct and indirect taxes vary substantially.

160.2 Professional members working in tax must comply with the fundamental principles of behaviour outlined in the Professional Conduct in Relation to Taxation (PCRT). It is beyond the scope of this *Code* to deal with detailed ethical issues relating to taxation services encountered by members. The guidance that follows consists therefore of general principles for members which apply to both direct and indirect taxation.

160.3 A member providing professional tax services has a duty to put forward the best position in favour of a client or an employer. However, the service must be carried out with professional competence, must not in any way impair integrity or objectivity and must be consistent with the law.

160.4 A member shall not hold out to a client or an employer the assurance that any tax return prepared and tax advice offered are beyond challenge. Instead the member shall ensure that the client or the employer is aware of the limitation attaching to tax advice and services so that they do not misinterpret an expression of opinion as an assertion of fact.

160.5 A member shall only undertake taxation work on the basis of full disclosure by the client or employer. The member, in dealing with the tax authorities, must act in good faith and exercise care in relation to facts or information presented on behalf of the client or employer. It will normally be assumed that facts and information on which business tax computations are based were provided by the client or employer as the taxpayer, and the latter bears ultimate responsibility for the accuracy of the facts, information and tax computations. The member shall avoid assuming responsibility for the accuracy of facts, etc. outside his or her own knowledge.

160.6 When a member submits a tax return or tax computation for a taxpayer client or employer, the member is acting as an agent. The nature and responsibilities of the member's duties should be made clear to the client or employer, in the case of the former, by a letter of engagement.

160.7 Tax advice or opinions of material consequence given to a client or an employer shall be recorded, either in the form of a letter or in a memorandum for the files.

160.8 In the case of a member in practice acting for a client, the member shall furnish copies of all tax computations to the client before submitting them to HMRC.

160.9 When a member learns of a material error or omission in a tax return of a prior year, or of a failure to file a required tax return, the member has a responsibility to advise promptly the client or employer of the error or omission and recommend that disclosure be made to HMRC. If the client or employer, after having had a reasonable time to reflect, does not correct the error, the member shall inform the client or employer in writing that it is not possible for the member to act for them in connection with that return or other related information submitted to the authorities. Funds dishonestly retained after discovery of an error or omission become criminal property and their retention amounts to money laundering by the client or employer. It is also a criminal offence in the UK for a person, including an accountant, to become concerned in an arrangement which he knows or suspects facilitates (by whatever means) the acquisition, retention, use or control of criminal property by or on behalf of another person. Other EU states have equivalent provisions. In each of these situations, the member shall comply with the duty to report the client's or employer's activities to the relevant authority, as explained in the following paragraphs.

160.10 A Licensed member whose client refuses to make disclosure of an error or omission to HMRC, after having had notice of it and a reasonable time to reflect, is obliged to report the client's refusal and the facts surrounding it to the MLRO if the member is within a firm, or to the appropriate authority (NCA in the UK) if the member is a sole practitioner. The member shall not disclose to the client or anyone else that such a report has been made if the member knows or suspects that to do so would be likely to prejudice any investigation which might be conducted following the report.

160.11 In circumstances where the employer of a member in business refuses to make disclosure of an error or omission to HMRC:

- where the employed member in business has acted in relation to the error or omission, he or she should report the employer's refusal and the surrounding facts, including the extent of the member's involvement, to the appropriate authority as soon as possible, as this may provide the member with a defence to the offence of facilitating the retention of criminal property

- where the employed member in business has not acted in relation to the error or omission, he or she is not obliged to report the matter to the authorities. However, if the member does make a report to the appropriate authority, such report will not amount to a breach of the member's duty of confidentiality.

160.12 Where a member in business is a contractor who is a 'relevant person' for the purposes of the *Money Laundering Regulations* in the UK or equivalent legislation in another EU State or other overseas jurisdictions, the member shall act in accordance with paragraph 160.10 above, as though he were a Licensed member. However, where the member in business is not a 'relevant person', he should act in accordance with paragraph 160.11 above.

160.13 All members have a responsibility to make themselves familiar with anti-money laundering and terrorist financing legislation and any guidance issued by AAT in this regard.

160.14 The tax authorities in many countries have extensive powers to obtain information. Members confronted by the exercise of these powers by the relevant authorities should seek appropriate legal advice.